The History of

The Patron Saint and the Birth of a Republic

Copyright © 2023 by Francesca Luise Rossi and Einar Felix Hansen.

All rights reserved. No part of this publication may be reproduced, stored in a retrieval system, or transmitted, in any form or by any means, electronic, mechanical, photocopying, recording, or otherwise, without the prior written permission of the copyright holder. This book was created with the help of Artificial Intelligence technology.

The contents of this book are intended for entertainment purposes only. While every effort has been made to ensure the accuracy and reliability of the information presented, the author and publisher make no warranties or representations as to the accuracy, completeness, or suitability of the information contained herein. The information presented in this book is not intended as a substitute for professional advice, and readers should consult with qualified professionals in the relevant fields for specific advice.

The Enigmatic Origins: San Marino's Ancient Beginnings 7

The Early Settlements: Tracing San Marino's Prehistoric Roots 10

The Founding of the Republic: The Birth of a Unique Nation 13

Ancient Governance: Unraveling the Early Political System 16

Fortifications and Defense: The Art of Protecting San Marino 19

Medieval Expansion: Spreading Influence Beyond Borders 22

Cultural Crossroads: San Marino's Encounter with Different Civilizations 25

Saint Marinus: The Patron Saint and National Icon 28

The Monastic Influence: Monasteries and their Role in Shaping the Country 31

Feuds and Alliances: San Marino amidst Regional Conflicts 34

The Republic's Constitution: The Evolution of a Unique Legal System 37

Art and Architecture: San Marino's Aesthetic Heritage 40

Trade and Commerce: The Economic Growth of a Mountain Republic 44

Challenging Times: Surviving Medieval Turmoil 48

The Renaissance Era: A Blossom of Artistic and Intellectual Achievements 51

The Titan of San Marino: Examining the Legendary Giambattista Belluzzi 54

A Glimpse into Daily Life: Traditions and Customs of the Past 57

The Secret of Longevity: How San Marino Maintained its Independence 60

The Grand Council: Aspects of Early Republican Government 63

The Changing Tides: Adapting to the Modern World 66

Literary Treasures: San Marino's Contributions to the Written Word 69

Chasing Freedom: San Marino's Role in the Struggle for Liberation 72

Rise of the Captains Regents: An Era of Dual Leadership 75

From Monarchy to Republic: The Transitional Phases 78

San Marino's Natural World: Wildlife and Ecology 81

A Taste of San Marino: Exploring the Country's Unique Cuisine 84

Tourist Delights: Must-Visit Sights and Attractions 87

City of Liberty: Exploring San Marino City's Historic Significance 91

Montegiardino: Unraveling the Charms of the Oldest Municipality 94

Borgo Maggiore: Tracing the Growth of an Ancient Village 97

Fiorentino: A Tapestry of Heritage and Legends 100

Acquaviva: Preserving the Medieval Essence 103

Serravalle: Where Nature Meets History 106

Conclusion 109

The Enigmatic Origins: San Marino's Ancient Beginnings

Nestled amidst the Apennine Mountains, the origins of San Marino remain shrouded in mystery, making it a fascinating subject of historical exploration. Situated on the northeastern coast of the Italian Peninsula, San Marino is renowned for being one of the world's oldest republics, boasting an unbroken continuity of governance that dates back to ancient times.

The story of San Marino's beginnings is intertwined with the life of its revered patron saint, Saint Marinus. According to legend, Saint Marinus, a Christian stonemason, fled the Roman Empire during the reign of Emperor Diocletian in the early 4th century. Seeking refuge from the intense persecution of Christians, he embarked on a journey to the rugged mountains, seeking a haven for his faith.

In the midst of the rocky terrain, Saint Marinus found solace atop Mount Titano, where he established a small community that would eventually become the foundation of the modern-day Republic of San Marino. The year of this establishment is believed to be 301 AD, marking the formal beginning of San Marino's unique history.

The Republic's status as an independent entity was further solidified in the years that followed, with a distinctive governance system taking shape. It developed a constitutional framework that emphasized communal decision-making and egalitarian principles, setting it apart from the prevailing monarchical structures of the time.

San Marino's early years were marked by its relative isolation and self-sufficiency, a key factor in maintaining its autonomy throughout the centuries. The surrounding mountains provided a natural barrier against potential invaders and external influence, enabling the fledgling community to thrive and develop its own distinct identity.

Historical records from the 5th and 6th centuries reveal that San Marino resisted various attempts of conquest by larger neighboring powers, including the Ostrogoths and the Byzantines. The Republic's ability to withstand such pressures further reinforced its status as a symbol of resilience and independence.

In the centuries that followed, San Marino experienced a steady expansion of its territory, incorporating nearby settlements and villages into its fold. The growing population and the development of trade routes brought about economic prosperity, enabling the Republic to establish diplomatic ties with neighboring cities and regions.

By the early Middle Ages, San Marino's unique status as a republic had become more widely recognized. Diplomatic documents from the 10th and 11th centuries referred to it as the "Land of the Saint," underlining its association with Saint Marinus and its commitment to Christian principles.

Despite its relatively small size, San Marino played a crucial role in mediating conflicts between warring factions in the region, earning a reputation as a neutral and impartial arbiter. This role contributed to its stability and earned respect from its larger neighbors.

Over time, the governance structure evolved to include a system of elected leaders, known as Captains Regents, who acted as the ceremonial heads of state and shared executive powers. This innovative political arrangement allowed for continuity and ensured the peaceful transfer of power within the Republic.

Throughout the medieval period, San Marino maintained its independence amid the constant geopolitical shifts of the Italian Peninsula. It skillfully navigated through wars, alliances, and territorial disputes, always safeguarding its autonomy and unique identity.

The Renaissance period brought a cultural renaissance to San Marino as well, with the flourishing of arts and scholarship. Though not as prominent as other Italian city-states, San Marino still contributed to the wider intellectual exchange of the time, leaving a mark in various fields.

As centuries passed, the enigmatic origins of San Marino's ancient beginnings have continued to intrigue historians and visitors alike. The legacy of Saint Marinus and the early settlers endures in the present-day, shaping the identity of this remarkable mountain republic.

Today, as we look back on the enigmatic origins of San Marino, we find a nation that has withstood the test of time, preserving its ancient roots and embodying the spirit of independence and resilience that has defined it for centuries. The story of San Marino's ancient beginnings serves as a testament to the enduring power of human determination and the pursuit of liberty, inspiring generations to come.

The Early Settlements: Tracing San Marino's Prehistoric Roots

The prehistoric origins of San Marino offer a captivating glimpse into the distant past of this small but significant republic. Long before the establishment of its renowned political system and the veneration of its patron saint, Saint Marinus, the land that would become San Marino bore witness to the presence of ancient communities and early settlers.

Archaeological evidence reveals that the territory of present-day San Marino was inhabited as far back as the Neolithic period, around 4,500 BCE. Excavations at various sites across the region have uncovered artifacts such as pottery, stone tools, and burial sites, offering valuable insights into the daily life and customs of these ancient inhabitants.

During the Bronze Age, which spanned from around 2200 BCE to 800 BCE, the area experienced further settlement and development. The transition from stone tools to bronze implements brought about advancements in agriculture, trade, and craftsmanship. This era saw the emergence of more organized societies, laying the groundwork for the region's future growth and complexity.

In the Iron Age, around 800 BCE to 200 BCE, the inhabitants of the region continued to develop their social structures and trading networks. Iron tools and weapons further improved their daily lives and defense capabilities, enabling them to navigate the challenges posed by their surroundings, including the rugged Apennine landscape.

The pre-Roman period witnessed a gradual integration of the San Marino area into the broader cultural sphere of the Italian Peninsula. While not a major center of ancient civilization like Rome or Pompeii, the region played a significant role in the interconnected network of tribes and settlements that characterized pre-Roman Italy.

The arrival of the Etruscans, an advanced civilization that dominated parts of central and northern Italy, also left its mark on the territory. Etruscan influences on art, architecture, and burial practices have been discovered in archaeological findings, underscoring the interconnectedness of the region with its neighboring communities.

By the 3rd century BCE, the Romans had begun their expansion across the Italian Peninsula, and the San Marino area came under their influence. Roman artifacts, including coins and inscriptions, have been uncovered, suggesting a gradual assimilation of local communities into the Roman cultural and administrative system.

The subsequent Romanization of the region brought about significant changes, with the construction of roads, infrastructure, and public buildings. The prosperous trade routes facilitated the exchange of goods and ideas, contributing to the region's growth and prosperity.

With the fall of the Western Roman Empire in the 5th century CE, the region experienced a period of uncertainty and upheaval. It faced invasions and migrations of various Germanic tribes, such as the Goths and the Lombards, which disrupted the established order and caused widespread disarray.

It was amidst this backdrop of societal upheaval that the legendary figure of Saint Marinus found refuge in the rugged mountains. His flight from the Roman persecution and subsequent establishment of a small community on Mount Titano marked the beginning of the unique and enduring history of San Marino.

The early settlements of San Marino were likely characterized by their self-sufficiency and isolation, given the challenging terrain that surrounded them. The mountainous landscape served as a natural defense, providing a measure of protection against external threats and fostering a sense of collective identity among the inhabitants.

While historical records from this period are scarce, oral traditions and local legends have helped preserve elements of San Marino's prehistoric roots. The early settlers' reverence for the land and their ability to adapt to their environment laid the foundation for the future development of a distinct society and governance system.

The Founding of the Republic: The Birth of a Unique Nation

The founding of the Republic of San Marino marks a pivotal moment in history, as it laid the groundwork for the birth of one of the world's oldest and most enduring nations. Rooted in the legend of Saint Marinus, this small but remarkable republic emerged as a beacon of independence and freedom in the midst of a tumultuous medieval world.

The year was 301 AD when Saint Marinus, a Christian stonemason, sought refuge from the widespread persecution of Christians in the Roman Empire. Fleeing the oppressive policies of Emperor Diocletian, he sought sanctuary in the rugged Apennine Mountains, ultimately finding solace atop Mount Titano. Here, in this remote and isolated location, Saint Marinus established a small community that would lay the foundation for the Republic of San Marino.

The early settlement on Mount Titano was characterized by its collective governance structure, where decisions were made through communal participation. This communal approach to decision-making would become a defining feature of the emerging republic and set it apart from the prevailing monarchical systems of the time.

Over time, the community on Mount Titano expanded and incorporated nearby settlements and villages, solidifying its presence and influence in the region. Although it remained relatively isolated from the major power centers of medieval Europe, the Republic of San Marino maintained amicable relations with neighboring regions and cities.

The unique political system of San Marino evolved into a quasi-republican governance model, with a commitment to individual freedom and civic participation. This experiment in self-governance captured the imaginations of its inhabitants, empowering them to take ownership of their destiny and maintain a sense of independence.

The establishment of the Republic of San Marino occurred during a period of significant social and political upheaval. The Roman Empire was in decline, and the European continent was fragmented into various kingdoms and feudal territories. In contrast, San Marino's determination to preserve its autonomy and democratic principles stood as an inspiring anomaly in an era of power struggles and territorial expansion.

The Republic's status as a self-governing entity was formalized in a series of documents, including the "Leges Statutae Republicae Sancti Marini," the foundational statute of San Marino, written in Latin during the 14th century. This statute outlined the principles of governance and the rights and responsibilities of the citizens, affirming the unique character of the republic.

Through diplomatic negotiations and skillful diplomacy, San Marino secured recognition of its independence from neighboring powers, further consolidating its position as a distinct nation in the medieval world. The papacy, in particular, acknowledged the sovereignty of the Republic, fostering a close and enduring relationship that has persisted to the present day.

San Marino's unique status as a republic during the medieval period allowed for a remarkable continuity of governance, a testament to the stability and adaptability of its political system. The periodic election of Captains Regents, the ceremonial heads of state, ensured a peaceful transfer of power and maintained the democratic ethos of the republic.

The Republic of San Marino also demonstrated a commitment to the protection of individual rights and liberties, making it a haven for those seeking refuge from religious or political persecution. This legacy of sheltering the oppressed reflects the compassion and empathy that have been central to the country's identity throughout its history.

Throughout the centuries, San Marino faced its share of challenges and external threats, but it weathered them with tenacity and unity. The geographic advantage of its mountainous terrain, coupled with the resilience of its people, fortified the Republic against potential invaders and allowed it to maintain its cherished independence.

San Marino's cultural and intellectual contributions during the medieval period were notable, despite its size and relative isolation. The republic fostered an environment conducive to creativity and scholarship, with notable contributions to literature, arts, and the sciences.

The founding of the Republic of San Marino was not only a historical event but also a philosophical statement on the value of freedom and collective governance. The principles of liberty and self-determination, rooted in its early beginnings, have endured and shaped the republic's identity to the present day.

Ancient Governance: Unraveling the Early Political System

The early political system of the Republic of San Marino provides a fascinating glimpse into the unique governance structure that emerged during ancient times. Rooted in the legend of Saint Marinus and the communal traditions of its early settlers, the system of governance in San Marino was a departure from the prevailing monarchical models of the medieval world.

At the heart of the ancient governance system in San Marino was the concept of communal decision-making. The community on Mount Titano, led by Saint Marinus, embraced a collective approach to governance, where important decisions were made through the participation of its citizens. This democratic ethos, established from its earliest days, set San Marino apart from other medieval entities that were governed by absolute rulers.

The governance structure was marked by the involvement of ordinary citizens in shaping the direction of the republic. The establishment of the Grand and General Council, composed of representatives from each family in San Marino, reflected the inclusive nature of its political system. This council served as the legislative body and played a crucial role in policy-making and law enforcement.

The Grand and General Council convened in the Arengo, an assembly that allowed citizens to voice their opinions and concerns freely. The Arengo was not only a platform for political discussions but also a symbol of the Republic's commitment to open dialogue and public engagement in decision-making.

As the Republic of San Marino expanded its territorial boundaries by incorporating nearby settlements and villages, the governance system adapted to accommodate the changing demographics. With the inclusion of new communities, the Grand and General Council saw an expansion in its representation, reflecting the commitment to maintaining an inclusive and equitable political system.

The Council of the Forty, an important institution in the early political system, served as an executive body tasked with executing the decisions of the Grand and General Council. Comprising four members from each of the country's castles (historical administrative divisions), the Council of the Forty was responsible for implementing laws and ensuring the smooth functioning of the republic.

The Captains Regents were another crucial element of the early political system. Elected by the Grand and General Council, the Captains Regents were the ceremonial heads of state and held executive powers. Their term of office was relatively short, usually lasting six months, to prevent the accumulation of excessive power and maintain a rotation of leadership.

The Captains Regents symbolized the principle of collegiality in San Marino's governance. Their joint rule underscored the idea that power was not concentrated in a single individual but shared among multiple leaders, minimizing the risk of tyranny and promoting collective decision-making.

San Marino's early political system was not devoid of external influences. Throughout the medieval period, the Republic faced diplomatic and political challenges from neighboring powers seeking to expand their territories. Yet, through skillful diplomacy and negotiation, San Marino managed to maintain its independence and political autonomy.

The continuity of the ancient governance system is remarkable. Even as the world around it evolved and experienced dramatic political changes, San Marino remained committed to its founding principles of democracy, self-governance, and civic engagement. This steadfast dedication to its unique political system has earned San Marino the distinction of being one of the world's oldest republics.

Throughout the centuries, the governance system of San Marino evolved, incorporating elements from the Renaissance and the Enlightenment eras, while still preserving its democratic foundation. Today, the Grand and General Council continues to be an essential pillar of the republic's political landscape, making it one of the rare examples of an ancient institution that endures in the modern world.

Fortifications and Defense: The Art of Protecting San Marino

The strategic location of San Marino amidst the rugged Apennine Mountains presented both advantages and challenges when it came to fortifications and defense. Throughout its long history, the Republic of San Marino recognized the importance of safeguarding its autonomy and independence, which led to the development of an intricate system of fortifications designed to protect its borders and people.

The early settlements on Mount Titano, founded by Saint Marinus in the 4th century AD, served as the genesis of the Republic of San Marino. Recognizing the need for protection, the early settlers began constructing rudimentary fortifications to defend their community against external threats.

The challenging terrain of the Apennines, with its steep cliffs and rocky outcrops, provided a natural advantage for the early settlers. These natural defenses made it difficult for potential invaders to approach Mount Titano easily. However, the inhabitants understood that relying solely on natural barriers was not sufficient to ensure the republic's safety.

Over the centuries, the fortifications evolved and expanded in response to changing military tactics and the evolving nature of warfare. Walls were erected around the settlements on Mount Titano, and watchtowers were strategically positioned to provide early warning of approaching enemies. These watchtowers not only served a defensive purpose but also facilitated communication among the different settlements within the republic.

One of the most significant fortifications in San Marino is the three iconic towers: Guaita, Cesta, and Montale. The Guaita Tower, the oldest of the three, was built in the 11th century and served as both a defensive structure and a prison. The Cesta Tower, constructed in the 13th century, housed the republic's weaponry and served as a lookout point. The Montale Tower, also from the 13th century, was a strategic fortification built on the highest point of Mount Titano.

The fortresses of San Marino were designed to withstand siege warfare, featuring thick stone walls and strategic positioning to maximize their defensive capabilities. During times of conflict, the republic's defenders would use the fortifications as vantage points to repel attackers and maintain a strategic advantage.

San Marino's commitment to fortifications and defense extended beyond the borders of Mount Titano. The republic constructed additional watchtowers and defensive structures in key locations throughout its territory, forming a network of fortified positions to deter potential invaders and maintain control over its expanding borders.

Despite its formidable fortifications, San Marino faced numerous challenges from neighboring powers throughout its history. Various medieval kingdoms and empires sought to annex the strategically positioned republic, recognizing its value as a stronghold in the Italian Peninsula.

San Marino's military defenses were not solely focused on external threats; the republic also recognized the importance of maintaining internal stability. The Captains Regents, the heads of state, had the authority to call upon citizens to defend the republic when necessary. This collective responsibility for defense fostered a strong sense of civic duty and unity among the population.

San Marino's unique status as a landlocked republic surrounded by powerful neighbors necessitated a delicate balance between military preparedness and diplomatic negotiations. The republic engaged in diplomatic efforts to secure alliances and establish mutually beneficial relationships, often leveraging its reputation as a neutral and impartial mediator in regional conflicts.

As the medieval period gave way to the Renaissance and beyond, San Marino's military needs evolved. The rise of firearms and artillery brought new challenges, prompting the republic to adapt its fortifications to withstand the changing nature of warfare.

In the modern era, San Marino's defense strategy shifted from fortifications and military might to international diplomacy and strategic alliances. The republic prioritized neutrality and peaceful coexistence with its neighbors, affirming its commitment to maintaining a reputation as a symbol of stability and diplomacy.

The fortifications of San Marino, including the iconic towers of Guaita, Cesta, and Montale, stand as enduring symbols of the republic's determination to protect its independence and sovereignty. Today, they serve as important historical landmarks, reminding visitors and residents alike of the rich and complex history of this extraordinary mountain republic.

Medieval Expansion: Spreading Influence Beyond Borders

The medieval period marked a significant phase of expansion for the Republic of San Marino, as it sought to extend its influence beyond the borders of its mountainous territory. Despite its small size, the republic's strategic positioning in the Italian Peninsula and its commitment to diplomacy allowed it to establish diplomatic ties with neighboring regions and cities.

San Marino's expansion during the medieval era was driven by several key factors. The republic's leaders recognized the importance of securing favorable trade agreements to bolster its economy and enhance its cultural exchange. This led to the establishment of trade routes and diplomatic missions to nearby cities and territories.

One of the earliest examples of San Marino's diplomatic efforts was the signing of a friendship treaty with the nearby city of Rimini in 1243. This treaty solidified the peaceful coexistence between the two regions and paved the way for future diplomatic engagements with other city-states.

Trade played a crucial role in San Marino's medieval expansion. The republic's strategic location along trade routes between northern and central Italy made it a valuable partner for merchants and traders. Through active engagement in trade, San Marino fostered economic ties with neighboring regions and contributed to the growth of its economy.

Moreover, San Marino's reputation as a neutral and impartial mediator in regional conflicts enhanced its standing among other city-states and kingdoms. The republic actively participated in peace negotiations, using its diplomatic skills to defuse tensions and facilitate dialogue between warring factions.

San Marino's efforts to spread its influence beyond its borders were not limited to mainland Italy. The republic established maritime trade with coastal cities in the Adriatic Sea, forging connections with seafaring communities and diversifying its economic endeavors.

As a testament to its diplomatic prowess, San Marino managed to secure a significant concession from Pope Urban VIII in 1631. The papal bull granted the republic extraterritorial rights to the Cava dei Balestrieri, a critical strategic location along the Adriatic coast. This concession further expanded San Marino's territorial influence and cemented its unique status as an independent entity with territorial possessions beyond its mountain borders.

Cultural exchange also played a significant role in San Marino's medieval expansion. The republic fostered an environment that welcomed scholars, artists, and intellectuals from neighboring regions, contributing to the flourishing of arts and sciences. San Marino's cultural influence spread through the exchange of ideas and artistic expressions, further enhancing its reputation as a center of intellectual exchange.

The preservation of its autonomy and democratic principles allowed San Marino to navigate the often turbulent political landscape of the medieval era successfully. While neighboring powers vied for territorial dominance, the republic's dedication to its core values ensured its independence and helped it avoid conflicts that could threaten its existence.

Throughout its expansion, San Marino maintained its identity as a republic rooted in the principles of democracy and self-governance. The election of Captains Regents, the collective decision-making in the Grand and General Council, and the inclusive nature of its governance system remained central to its medieval political landscape.

As the medieval period gave way to the Renaissance, San Marino's expansion continued to evolve. The republic further solidified its cultural exchange with other centers of learning and artistic expression in Italy, leaving an indelible mark on the broader intellectual landscape of the time.

Cultural Crossroads: San Marino's Encounter with Different Civilizations

Throughout its rich history, the Republic of San Marino has stood as a cultural crossroads, where different civilizations converged, exchanged ideas, and left their indelible marks on the nation's identity. Situated at the crossroads of the Italian Peninsula, San Marino became a hub for cultural interactions, fostering an environment that celebrated diversity and intellectual exchange.

One of the earliest influences on San Marino's cultural landscape was the Etruscans, an ancient civilization that dominated parts of central and northern Italy. Etruscan artifacts have been uncovered in archaeological excavations, highlighting their presence and early interactions with the region.

As the Roman Empire expanded its influence across the Italian Peninsula, San Marino fell under Roman rule and experienced Romanization. The influence of Roman culture is evident in the architectural remains, such as roads and bridges, that still dot the landscape. Roman artifacts, including coins and inscriptions, have also been discovered, providing further evidence of their cultural impact.

With the decline of the Western Roman Empire in the 5th century AD, the Italian Peninsula experienced waves of invasions and migrations from various Germanic tribes. The Lombards, in particular, settled in nearby regions and came into contact with San Marino. While there are no direct records of conflicts or interactions during this period, it is likely that the Lombards' presence influenced the cultural fabric of the republic.

In the medieval era, San Marino's strategic location attracted the attention of neighboring powers, including the Byzantine Empire and the Papal States. Byzantine influences on art and architecture have been noted in the region, particularly in the intricate mosaics and frescoes found in churches and historical buildings.

The Papal States, the temporal territory of the Pope, exerted both political and cultural influence on San Marino. Despite diplomatic tensions at times, the republic managed to maintain cordial relations with the papacy, with the Pope recognizing its autonomy in various documents and treaties.

San Marino's unique status as an independent republic allowed it to develop its distinctive cultural identity. While influenced by neighboring civilizations, the republic cultivated its traditions, customs, and arts, contributing to a rich tapestry of cultural expressions that set it apart from other Italian city-states.

The flourishing of arts and scholarship in San Marino during the Renaissance period further enhanced its role as a cultural crossroads. The republic attracted scholars, artists, and thinkers from neighboring regions, fostering an environment of intellectual exchange and creativity. Notable individuals, including renowned mathematician Luca Pacioli, found refuge and inspiration in the republic during this era.

San Marino's commitment to cultural exchange extended beyond its borders. The republic engaged in diplomatic and cultural missions, forging relationships with other European centers of learning and art. Its cultural ambassadors played an essential role in promoting the republic's values and artistic achievements on the international stage.

The advent of the printing press in the late medieval period facilitated the dissemination of knowledge and ideas. San Marino embraced this transformative technology, and the republic became a hub for the production and distribution of printed materials, further enhancing its reputation as a center of intellectual exchange.

Religious tolerance was another hallmark of San Marino's cultural landscape. The republic welcomed individuals fleeing religious persecution in neighboring regions, allowing them to practice their faith freely. This openness to diversity contributed to the enrichment of San Marino's cultural milieu.

The 18th and 19th centuries witnessed significant cultural transformations in San Marino, as the republic aligned its artistic expressions with the prevailing Neoclassical and Romantic movements of the time. Painters, poets, and musicians sought inspiration from the republic's landscapes and traditions, leaving their creative imprints on the nation's cultural heritage.

Saint Marinus: The Patron Saint and National Icon

Saint Marinus, the venerated patron saint of the Republic of San Marino, occupies a central place in the nation's history and identity. Rooted in legend and ancient traditions, the story of Saint Marinus has become intertwined with the founding and enduring spirit of the world's oldest republic.

According to historical accounts, Saint Marinus was born in the Roman city of Arba (modern-day Rab, Croatia) during the 3rd century AD. Little is known about his early life, but it is widely believed that he was a Christian stonemason who lived during the reign of Emperor Diocletian, a ruler notorious for his persecution of Christians.

In the face of intense persecution, Saint Marinus, like many other Christians of his time, sought refuge and freedom from religious oppression. Fleeing from Arba, he embarked on a journey that led him to the rugged Apennine Mountains in present-day San Marino. Upon reaching Mount Titano, Saint Marinus found solace and safety in its rocky cliffs and dense forests. It was atop this mountain that he established a small Christian community, which would eventually evolve into the Republic of San Marino.

The year 301 AD is traditionally considered the formal beginning of San Marino's history, marking the establishment of Saint Marinus' small settlement on Mount Titano. The saint's commitment to religious freedom and the values of Christianity would lay the foundation for the unique political system and cultural identity that developed over the centuries.

Saint Marinus' reputation as a pious and virtuous individual grew, and he became a revered figure among his followers and the local inhabitants. The fledgling community on Mount Titano, recognizing the significance of their spiritual leader, came to regard him as their patron and protector.

In the centuries that followed, devotion to Saint Marinus deepened, and his memory became an integral part of the republic's collective consciousness. His legacy as a symbol of freedom, resilience, and moral fortitude provided inspiration to the citizens of San Marino as they navigated through the challenges of history.

Throughout the medieval era, Saint Marinus' status as the patron saint of San Marino was further solidified. The republic's religious and political leaders sought to honor his memory and ensure his enduring influence on the nation. The Feast of Saint Marinus, celebrated on September 3rd, became an important annual event, commemorating his life and the founding of the republic.

Legend and folklore surrounding Saint Marinus further embellished his story and contributed to the development of a distinct national identity for San Marino. Various accounts of miraculous interventions and divine protection attributed to the saint added to his veneration and reinforced his role as a symbol of hope and divine intercession.

As San Marino's reputation as a neutral and impartial mediator in regional conflicts grew, so did Saint Marinus' symbolic association with peacemaking and diplomatic efforts. The republic's dedication to preserving peace and avoiding armed conflicts found resonance in the values embodied by their patron saint.

San Marino's religious freedom and tolerance, partly inspired by Saint Marinus' commitment to the values of Christianity, allowed the republic to welcome individuals of various faiths and beliefs. The nation's commitment to protecting the rights of religious minorities further exemplified the enduring legacy of its patron saint.

In art and iconography, Saint Marinus has been depicted in various forms, often portrayed as a bearded figure wearing the vestments of a Christian saint. Images of him holding a model of Mount Titano or the republic's coat of arms serve as powerful reminders of his central role in San Marino's history and identity.

The devotion to Saint Marinus extends beyond the borders of San Marino. He is recognized as a saint in the Roman Catholic Church and is venerated by Christians worldwide. In addition to his role as the patron saint of San Marino, he is also regarded as the patron saint of those seeking refuge, protection, and spiritual guidance.

Today, Saint Marinus remains an essential national icon and a symbol of the republic's enduring commitment to freedom, democracy, and peaceful coexistence. The legacy of this humble stonemason, who sought refuge on a mountain peak, continues to inspire generations and shape the character of the world's oldest republic. The story of Saint Marinus stands as a testament to the transformative power of faith, courage, and the pursuit of liberty that defines the remarkable history of the Republic of San Marino.

The Monastic Influence: Monasteries and their Role in Shaping the Country

The monastic influence in the Republic of San Marino played a significant role in shaping the country's religious, cultural, and educational landscape. Monasteries served as centers of spirituality, learning, and communal life, leaving a lasting imprint on the development of this ancient republic.

During the medieval period, monastic communities were prevalent across Europe, and San Marino was no exception. Monasticism, characterized by a life of dedication to prayer, contemplation, and communal living, became an essential aspect of religious life in the region.

Monasteries in San Marino were founded primarily by religious orders from neighboring regions. These monastic communities brought with them not only their religious practices but also their knowledge and expertise in various fields, including agriculture, medicine, and arts.

One of the most prominent monasteries in San Marino was the Monastery of Santa Clara, founded in the 13th century by the Order of Saint Clare. This female Franciscan community played a crucial role in the spiritual and social life of the republic, providing refuge for women seeking a life of religious devotion and community service.

Another significant monastery was the Monastery of San Francesco, established by the Franciscan Order in the 14th century. The Franciscans' dedication to poverty, humility, and service to the poor resonated with the values of the republic, making the Monastery of San Francesco a center of spiritual guidance and charity.

The monastic communities in San Marino were not isolated entities; they actively engaged with the broader society and contributed to the cultural enrichment of the republic. Monks and nuns in these communities played pivotal roles as teachers, scholars, and artists, fostering an environment of intellectual exchange and creativity.

The monasteries in San Marino were instrumental in preserving and disseminating knowledge during a time when books were scarce and education was limited. Monks and nuns transcribed and copied ancient manuscripts, safeguarding important texts from the perils of time and war.

The monastic libraries became repositories of knowledge, attracting scholars and seekers of wisdom from neighboring regions. Monastic scriptoria produced beautiful illuminated manuscripts, showcasing the artistic talents of the scribes and enriching the cultural heritage of San Marino.

The monasteries also played a crucial role in providing healthcare to the local population. Monastic infirmaries offered medical assistance and care to the sick and injured, serving as early healthcare centers for the community.

San Marino's monastic communities actively engaged in charitable activities, serving the poor and vulnerable. The principles of compassion and service to others embodied by the religious orders resonated with the republic's commitment to social justice and communal welfare.

Over time, the influence of monasticism in San Marino expanded beyond religious and cultural spheres and extended into the political landscape. Some members of monastic orders held influential positions in the republic's government, contributing to its governance and administration.

However, as the world around San Marino changed, so did the role of monastic communities. The advent of the Renaissance and the rise of secular education shifted the center of learning from monasteries to universities and schools.

The Enlightenment era brought further changes, leading to the suppression of many monasteries across Europe, including some in San Marino. As the republic embraced the principles of secular governance and democratic values, the monastic influence waned, and the remaining monasteries shifted their focus to other religious and charitable activities.

Despite the decline in the number of monasteries in San Marino, their legacy endures in the cultural fabric of the republic. The architectural remains of these sacred spaces stand as testaments to the devotion and contributions of the monastic communities that once thrived within the republic's borders.

Today, the religious heritage of monasticism in San Marino continues to be celebrated and preserved. The Republic of San Marino recognizes the historical significance of its monastic past and cherishes the enduring impact of these spiritual communities on its religious, cultural, and educational heritage.

Feuds and Alliances: San Marino amidst Regional Conflicts

Throughout its long history, the Republic of San Marino found itself amidst a complex web of regional conflicts, navigating diplomatic challenges, and forging strategic alliances to preserve its autonomy and independence. Situated in the heart of the Italian Peninsula, the small mountain republic became a coveted territory for neighboring powers, leading to frequent feuds and diplomatic maneuvers.

In the medieval era, San Marino's strategic location attracted the attention of various regional powers, including neighboring city-states and duchies. The republic's commitment to maintaining its independence and democratic principles often brought it into conflict with ambitious rulers seeking to expand their territories.

One of the earliest feuds in San Marino's history was with the Malatesta family, rulers of the nearby city of Rimini. The Malatesta sought to assert their control over the region, leading to clashes with the republic. These conflicts, however, did not result in the annexation of San Marino, thanks to the republic's determined defense and diplomatic efforts.

The papacy also played a significant role in regional conflicts involving San Marino. The Pope recognized the strategic importance of the republic and sought to maintain friendly relations with it. At times, the Papal States served as a protectorate for San Marino, offering support and diplomatic assistance during periods of external threats.

In the 15th century, San Marino faced a formidable adversary in the form of the Borgias, a powerful and ambitious family that dominated the Papal States. The Borgias sought to subdue the republic and establish their control over it. However, through skillful diplomacy and military resistance, San Marino managed to maintain its autonomy.

The Republic of San Marino's ability to preserve its independence during times of regional turmoil was not solely reliant on military strength; it was equally dependent on diplomatic astuteness. The republic's leaders engaged in shrewd negotiations, forming alliances with neighboring powers, and seeking mutual interests to protect their nation's sovereignty.

During the Italian Wars of the 16th century, the republic managed to maintain its neutrality, despite being surrounded by warring factions. The strategic decision to remain impartial allowed San Marino to avoid devastating conflicts that ravaged other regions of Italy.

The 17th and 18th centuries brought new challenges as San Marino confronted external threats from various European powers. The republic, however, skillfully navigated these challenges, employing a blend of diplomacy and defensive strategies to safeguard its borders and maintain its autonomy.

In the 19th century, the unification of Italy presented a unique set of challenges for San Marino. The republic sought to maintain its independence while surrounded by a newly unified Italian state. Through careful negotiations, San Marino secured its status as an independent state within the unified Italy, ensuring its distinct identity and territorial integrity.

World War II brought unprecedented challenges to San Marino. The republic faced pressure from both Fascist Italy and Nazi Germany, which sought to annex the small nation. However, San Marino's long-standing policy of neutrality and its commitment to humanitarian principles allowed it to avoid direct involvement in the war.

During the Cold War era, San Marino continued to uphold its neutrality, refraining from aligning with either NATO or the Warsaw Pact. This principled stance solidified the republic's reputation as a symbol of peace and non-alignment on the global stage.

In modern times, San Marino's foreign policy focuses on promoting peace, stability, and cooperation in international affairs. The republic actively participates in various diplomatic forums, advocating for global issues such as human rights, disarmament, and environmental protection.

The Republic's Constitution: The Evolution of a Unique Legal System

The Republic of San Marino boasts a remarkable legal system with a long and evolving history. Rooted in ancient communal traditions and democratic principles, the republic's constitution has stood the test of time, shaping its governance and preserving its autonomy.

The earliest traces of San Marino's legal system can be traced back to the foundations of the republic in the 4th century AD. Saint Marinus and the early settlers on Mount Titano established a communal form of governance, where decisions were made collectively through the Grand and General Council. The principles of democracy and participatory decision-making laid the groundwork for the unique legal system of San Marino. The Grand and General Council served as the legislative body, passing laws and making crucial policy decisions for the republic.

As the republic expanded its territorial boundaries and incorporated nearby settlements, the governance system adapted to accommodate the changing demographics. The Grand and General Council saw an expansion in its representation, becoming a reflection of the republic's commitment to inclusivity and equitable representation. In the 13th century, the Statuti, or the first written laws, were established. The Statuti codified the customary practices and laws that had been in place for centuries, providing a legal framework for the republic's governance. This marked a significant step in the formalization of San Marino's legal system.

The Statuti governed various aspects of daily life in the republic, including property rights, civil disputes, criminal offenses, and trade regulations. They emphasized the principles of justice, fairness, and respect for individual rights, laying the foundation for the republic's commitment to the rule of law. Throughout the medieval era, San Marino's legal system evolved in response to changing political and social dynamics. Amendments and additions to the Statuti reflected the republic's ability to adapt to new challenges while preserving its core values.

The legal system of San Marino also drew inspiration from other legal traditions of the time, including Roman law and Canon law. The republic's geographic proximity to the Papal States and its historical ties to the Roman Empire influenced the development of its legal principles.

One of the significant components of San Marino's legal system is the Captains Regents. Elected every six months, the Captains Regents serve as the ceremonial heads of state and hold executive powers. Their dual leadership ensures a rotation of authority, preventing the concentration of power in a single individual.

The Council of the Forty, established in the 13th century, served as an executive body responsible for implementing laws and overseeing the administration of the republic. Composed of representatives from each castle (administrative division), the Council of the Forty played a crucial role in maintaining the republic's stability and efficient governance.

Over the centuries, the Statuti continued to be revised and updated to reflect the changing needs of the republic. The republic's commitment to preserving its autonomy and democratic principles remained a guiding force in the evolution of its legal system.

In the 19th century, the Statuti underwent significant reforms to adapt to the modern era. The introduction of a written constitution in 1865 formalized the structure of the republic's government and legal system, reaffirming its democratic character.

The constitution of 1865 established the separation of powers among the Grand and General Council, the Captains Regents, and the Council of the Forty. It also enshrined the principles of human rights and individual freedoms, emphasizing the republic's commitment to upholding the dignity and liberty of its citizens.

In modern times, the legal system of San Marino continues to evolve, adapting to the demands of the contemporary world while preserving its centuries-old traditions. The republic's commitment to the rule of law and democratic governance remains steadfast, providing a stable foundation for its continued growth and development.

The legal system of the Republic of San Marino stands as a testament to the enduring power of democratic principles and the pursuit of justice. Rooted in ancient communal traditions, shaped by historical influences, and formalized through written laws and constitutions, it reflects the resilience and adaptability of a nation that has successfully preserved its autonomy and unique identity throughout the ages. The evolution of San Marino's legal system is a living testament to the triumph of democratic governance and the enduring quest for justice and liberty in a world shaped by changing political and social landscapes.

Art and Architecture: San Marino's Aesthetic Heritage

The Republic of San Marino boasts a rich aesthetic heritage, with a diverse array of art and architectural treasures that span centuries of history. Rooted in the influences of neighboring regions and shaped by the republic's unique identity, San Marino's art and architecture stand as a testament to its cultural significance and artistic achievements.

In the early centuries of its existence, San Marino's artistic expressions were primarily religious in nature. The rise of Christianity in the region led to the construction of numerous churches and religious buildings, showcasing the prevailing architectural styles of the time.

One of the most significant religious structures in San Marino is the Basilica of San Marino, dedicated to the republic's patron saint. This Romanesque-style church dates back to the 19th century and is an important pilgrimage site for both locals and visitors.

The Basilica's façade, adorned with intricate stone carvings and a rose window, showcases the architectural craftsmanship of the era. Its interior features exquisite frescoes and religious artworks that depict scenes from the life of Saint Marinus and other religious figures.

Another prominent religious site is the Church of San Francesco, founded in the 14th century by the Franciscan Order. This church exemplifies the architectural transition from Romanesque to Gothic styles, with its pointed arches, ribbed vaults, and flying buttresses.

Throughout the medieval period, San Marino's religious buildings continued to evolve, incorporating elements of Romanesque, Gothic, and later Renaissance styles. The Church of Santa Chiara, founded by the Order of Saint Clare, features splendid frescoes that reflect the artistic achievements of the Renaissance period.

San Marino's medieval architecture is not limited to religious buildings; the republic's defensive fortifications also boast impressive structures that showcase the military and architectural prowess of the time. The Three Towers of San Marino, located on Mount Titano, are iconic symbols of the republic and have been recognized as UNESCO World Heritage Sites.

The First Tower, also known as the Guaita, is the oldest and the most famous of the three. Built in the 11th century, it served as a watchtower and a fortress to protect the republic from external threats. The Second Tower, or the Cesta, was added in the 13th century and served both military and administrative purposes.

The Third Tower, or the Montale, is the smallest of the three and was constructed in the 14th century. Its primary function was as a prison, housing captives during times of conflict. Together, the Three Towers form a striking architectural ensemble that symbolizes the republic's commitment to defending its independence.

The Renaissance period brought a flourishing of arts and culture in San Marino. The republic became a haven for artists and scholars seeking refuge from conflicts in neighboring regions. Artists like Federico Zuccari and Domenico di Pace Beccafumi found inspiration in San Marino, leaving their artistic imprints on various buildings and artworks.

The Palazzo Pubblico, the seat of the republic's government, is an architectural gem that reflects the influences of the Renaissance period. Its elegant façade features decorative elements and artistic details that embody the republic's appreciation for beauty and aesthetics.

The Palazzo Pergami Belluzzi, built in the 17th century, showcases the transition from Renaissance to Baroque architectural styles. Its elaborate façade and ornate decorations exemplify the opulence and grandeur of the Baroque era.

The 18th and 19th centuries witnessed a revival of classicism in San Marino's architecture. Neoclassical influences became evident in buildings like the Teatro Titano, a theater built in the early 19th century, which featured columns, porticos, and other classical elements.

The republic's commitment to preserving its architectural heritage has resulted in the restoration and conservation of many historical buildings. The San Marino Historic Center, with its cobbled streets and charming medieval houses, has been recognized as a UNESCO World Heritage Site, ensuring the preservation of its architectural legacy for future generations.

San Marino's art heritage extends beyond architecture to encompass a diverse range of artistic expressions. The republic has produced talented painters, sculptors, and artisans whose works have left a lasting impact on the art world.

In the modern era, San Marino continues to foster a vibrant artistic community, with numerous galleries, museums, and cultural centers showcasing the works of contemporary artists. The republic's commitment to the arts is evident in various cultural events and festivals that celebrate creativity and artistic expression.

Trade and Commerce: The Economic Growth of a Mountain Republic

The Republic of San Marino, nestled in the Apennine Mountains, has a storied history of trade and commerce that spans centuries. Despite its small size and mountainous terrain, the republic's strategic location along important trade routes and its enterprising spirit allowed it to flourish economically and play a significant role in regional and international trade.

San Marino's earliest trade activities can be traced back to its inception in the 4th century AD. As the republic's population grew, trade became an essential means of sustenance and economic growth for its citizens. The rugged landscape, while challenging for agricultural pursuits, provided access to valuable resources, such as timber and stone, which became commodities for trade.

During the medieval era, San Marino established trading relationships with neighboring regions and city-states. Its unique political status as an independent republic enabled it to engage in commerce with different powers without being subject to the taxes and restrictions imposed by larger kingdoms.

The republic's proximity to the Adriatic Sea facilitated maritime trade, with San Marino's merchants establishing trading posts and maritime routes along the coast. The port of Rimini, in particular, served as a vital link for San Marino's trade connections to the wider Mediterranean region.

San Marino's enterprising merchants ventured beyond regional boundaries and engaged in long-distance trade with other European centers. The republic's exports included agricultural products, textiles, leather goods, and ceramics, while imports comprised luxury goods, spices, and valuable commodities.

In the 13th and 14th centuries, San Marino's thriving trade activities contributed to its economic prosperity and cultural exchange. The republic's reputation as a neutral and reliable trading partner attracted merchants from different regions, fostering an environment of economic cooperation and prosperity.

During the Renaissance period, the republic's trade networks expanded further, thanks to its active participation in the Italian commercial network. San Marino's merchants established trade relationships with major Italian cities, such as Venice, Florence, and Genoa, becoming key players in the flourishing trade between Italy and other European markets.

The republic's dedication to maintaining peace and neutrality allowed it to navigate through regional conflicts and trade disputes, safeguarding its economic interests and reputation as a reliable trading partner. The concept of diplomatic immunity, established by treaties with neighboring powers, further protected San Marino's merchants and assets during times of political instability.

As San Marino's influence and economic growth continued to expand, it faced competition and challenges from neighboring powers seeking to gain control of lucrative trade routes. Despite these pressures, the republic managed to preserve its economic independence through astute diplomacy and prudent economic policies.

The 18th and 19th centuries brought significant changes to the economic landscape of San Marino. The advent of the Industrial Revolution in neighboring regions transformed global trade dynamics, leading to the decline of traditional artisanal trades and the rise of industrial manufacturing.

San Marino's economy, traditionally based on crafts and agriculture, faced challenges in adapting to the changing economic climate. However, the republic's resilience and entrepreneurial spirit enabled it to explore new opportunities and industries, such as tourism and financial services.

In the 19th century, San Marino's banking sector experienced considerable growth, attracting deposits from foreign clients and becoming a key player in the global financial landscape. The republic's reputation for financial stability and secrecy made it an attractive destination for international clients seeking to safeguard their assets.

The 20th century brought further diversification to San Marino's economy. While traditional crafts and agriculture continued to be significant contributors, the republic expanded its industries to include electronics, telecommunications, and tourism.

San Marino's commitment to fostering a business-friendly environment and promoting innovation attracted foreign investment and multinational companies. The republic's tax incentives and economic policies incentivized entrepreneurs and businesses to establish a presence in its borders.

In recent decades, San Marino has embraced digital technology and e-commerce, further enhancing its position in the global economy. The republic's geographic location and advanced telecommunications infrastructure make it an ideal hub for digital businesses seeking access to European markets.

Today, San Marino continues to thrive as a dynamic and diverse economy, grounded in its centuries-old legacy of trade and commerce. The republic's commitment to free trade, economic diversification, and innovation ensures its continued economic growth and relevance on the global stage.

Challenging Times: Surviving Medieval Turmoil

The medieval period was a tumultuous time for the Republic of San Marino. Nestled in the Apennine Mountains, the small mountain republic faced numerous challenges and upheavals that tested its resilience and determination to preserve its autonomy and independence.

During the early medieval era, San Marino found itself amidst territorial disputes and conflicts with neighboring powers. The Malatesta family, rulers of the nearby city-state of Rimini, sought to expand their territories, leading to clashes with the republic. Despite facing superior military forces, San Marino's strategic location and well-defended fortifications allowed it to withstand external pressures.

In the 13th century, the republic faced a formidable adversary in the form of the Borgias, a powerful and ambitious family that dominated the Papal States. The Borgias sought to subdue San Marino and establish control over the mountain republic. However, through a combination of strategic alliances and military resistance, San Marino managed to maintain its autonomy.

Throughout the medieval era, San Marino navigated through the political complexities of the Italian Peninsula, which was divided into various city-states and feudal territories. The republic's commitment to neutrality and peaceful coexistence allowed it to avoid entanglement in the endless feuds and conflicts that plagued the region.

One of the most critical challenges during this period was the ongoing struggle for religious and political power. The Papal States, led by the Pope, sought to assert authority over the region and bring the republic under papal control. However, San Marino's leaders skillfully negotiated and maintained diplomatic relations with the papacy, preserving its status as an independent entity.

Despite the regional conflicts and challenges, San Marino's commitment to democratic principles and communal governance remained unwavering. The republic's Grand and General Council, composed of all male citizens, continued to play a central role in decision-making and policy formulation.

In the face of external threats, San Marino's citizens rallied together to defend their homeland. The republic's commitment to communal defense was a core tenet of its survival during these challenging times. The construction and fortification of the Three Towers, which served as defensive bastions on Mount Titano, symbolized the republic's determination to protect its autonomy.

The Statuti, the republic's first written laws, also played a crucial role in navigating through the medieval turmoil. The legal framework provided a foundation for the republic's governance, ensuring justice and fairness for its citizens and maintaining order during times of upheaval.

Despite its size, San Marino actively engaged in diplomatic efforts to secure peace and protect its interests. The republic's leaders established treaties and alliances with neighboring powers, demonstrating a keen understanding of the delicate balance of power in the region.

The republic's reputation for neutrality and fair dealing earned it the respect of other European powers, allowing it to maintain open channels of communication and trade with various regions. San Marino's merchants and diplomats built a network of connections that extended far beyond the borders of the Italian Peninsula.

While the medieval period was challenging, it also presented opportunities for growth and cultural exchange. San Marino became a haven for intellectuals and artists seeking refuge from conflicts in neighboring regions. The republic's vibrant cultural life flourished, leaving an indelible impact on the development of art, literature, and philosophy in the region.

As the medieval era drew to a close, San Marino's resilience and determination to survive through challenging times paved the way for its continued existence and relevance in the modern world. The republic's commitment to democracy, diplomacy, and economic diversification laid the foundation for its future growth and stability.

The Renaissance Era: A Blossom of Artistic and Intellectual Achievements

The Renaissance era marked a period of extraordinary cultural and intellectual flourishing in Europe, and the Republic of San Marino was no exception. As the winds of change swept across the Italian Peninsula, San Marino experienced a renaissance of its own, with artistic and intellectual achievements that left a lasting impact on its history and cultural heritage.

The Renaissance, which means "rebirth," emerged in Italy during the 14th century and continued into the 17th century. This remarkable period witnessed a revival of interest in the classical art, literature, and philosophy of ancient Greece and Rome. Humanism, a key philosophical movement, placed emphasis on the potential and capabilities of human beings, encouraging individualism and the pursuit of knowledge.

The geographic location of San Marino within Italy placed it at the heart of the Renaissance movement. The republic became a melting pot of ideas and artistic influences, attracting scholars, artists, and thinkers from neighboring regions and beyond.

The spirit of the Renaissance was embodied in San Marino's commitment to education and intellectual pursuit. The republic's leaders recognized the importance of knowledge and learning, and they actively promoted the study of humanities, arts, and sciences.

One of the most significant contributions of the Renaissance era to San Marino's cultural heritage was in the field of art. The republic became a haven for artists seeking refuge from political upheaval and religious conflicts in neighboring regions. Prominent artists such as Federico Zuccari and Domenico di Pace Beccafumi found inspiration in San Marino, creating masterpieces that adorn the republic's churches and buildings.

San Marino's religious buildings became canvases for Renaissance art, with frescoes and paintings depicting biblical scenes and religious figures. The Church of San Francesco, for instance, boasts stunning Renaissance frescoes that reflect the artistic achievements of the period.

The republic's commitment to the arts was not limited to visual arts alone; it also extended to literature and philosophy. San Marino's libraries and cultural centers became gathering places for scholars and thinkers, fostering an environment of intellectual exchange and innovation.

The Renaissance also left its mark on San Marino's architectural landscape. The republic's buildings and palaces reflected the influence of classical architectural styles, with elements such as columns, pilasters, and domes becoming prominent features in the design of civic and religious structures.

The Palazzo Pubblico, the seat of the republic's government, showcases a blend of Gothic and Renaissance architectural elements. Its façade features decorative details and sculptural elements that embody the artistic spirit of the era.

In addition to promoting artistic and intellectual achievements, the Renaissance era saw advancements in science and technology. San Marino's commitment to education extended to scientific pursuits, with scholars exploring various fields, including astronomy, mathematics, and medicine.

During the Renaissance, San Marino's reputation as a center of culture and learning extended beyond its borders. The republic's scholars and artists established connections with other European centers, contributing to the exchange of ideas and the dissemination of knowledge across the continent.

The Renaissance era in San Marino also witnessed the flourishing of humanist ideals and the appreciation for the individual's role in society. Humanist scholars emphasized the importance of education, civic engagement, and ethical conduct, shaping the republic's values and identity.

As the Renaissance era drew to a close, its legacy continued to inspire subsequent generations in San Marino and beyond. The republic's commitment to preserving its cultural heritage and promoting the arts remains evident in its museums, galleries, and cultural events that celebrate the achievements of the past and nurture creativity in the present.

The Titan of San Marino: Examining the Legendary Giambattista Belluzzi

Giambattista Belluzzi, a renowned figure in the history of the Republic of San Marino, was a man of remarkable intellect, ingenuity, and vision. Born in San Marino in 1525, he left an indelible mark on the republic's cultural, political, and architectural landscape.

From a young age, Belluzzi displayed exceptional talent and curiosity. His thirst for knowledge led him to pursue education in various fields, including architecture, engineering, and mathematics. His early training in these disciplines laid the foundation for his future accomplishments.

Belluzzi's architectural genius quickly earned him recognition in the republic and beyond. His innovative approach to design, blending classical and Renaissance elements, marked a departure from the prevailing architectural styles of the time. His works became a testament to the artistic and intellectual achievements of the Renaissance era in San Marino.

One of Belluzzi's most significant contributions to San Marino's architectural heritage was the design and construction of the Palazzo Pubblico. This grandiose structure, completed in 1884, served as the seat of the republic's government. Its elegant façade, adorned with sculptures and decorative details, reflected Belluzzi's artistic vision and attention to detail.

Inside the Palazzo Pubblico, Belluzzi created an environment that exuded grandeur and sophistication. Lavish frescoes and paintings adorned the walls and ceilings, depicting scenes from San Marino's history and celebrating its cultural identity.

Beyond the Palazzo Pubblico, Belluzzi's architectural prowess extended to other civic and religious buildings in San Marino. He designed and renovated numerous churches and palaces, leaving an architectural legacy that remains prominent in the republic's urban landscape.

Belluzzi's talents were not confined to architecture alone; he also excelled in engineering and city planning. His vision for urban development included the construction of aqueducts, bridges, and fortifications, further enhancing the republic's infrastructure and defense capabilities.

The fortifications on Mount Titano, which became known as the Three Towers of San Marino, were among Belluzzi's most ambitious engineering projects. He transformed these medieval structures into formidable defensive bastions, symbolizing the republic's commitment to safeguarding its autonomy.

Belluzzi's architectural achievements extended beyond the borders of San Marino. His reputation as a visionary architect and engineer attracted the attention of prominent figures in neighboring regions. He was sought after to consult on various architectural and engineering projects, and his expertise was highly regarded.

In addition to his architectural legacy, Belluzzi played a significant role in the republic's political life. His keen understanding of governance and diplomacy led him to serve in various administrative and diplomatic capacities. He was a member of the Council of the Forty and served as a diplomatic envoy to other European powers.

Belluzzi's political acumen and diplomatic skills proved invaluable in safeguarding San Marino's autonomy during a time of political turmoil in Italy. He navigated through complex regional dynamics, forging alliances and securing treaties that protected the republic's interests and independence.

As a humanist, Belluzzi also made significant contributions to the republic's cultural and intellectual life. He supported the establishment of educational institutions and libraries, nurturing an environment of learning and knowledge dissemination.

In his later years, Belluzzi focused on philanthropy and the welfare of his fellow citizens. He contributed to various charitable causes and supported the less fortunate, leaving a legacy of benevolence and compassion that endures to this day.

Giambattista Belluzzi's life and achievements stand as a testament to the power of intellect, creativity, and visionary leadership. His contributions to San Marino's architectural heritage, political stability, and cultural development have earned him the title of the "Titan of San Marino." His legacy continues to inspire future generations, reminding them of the transformative potential of individual brilliance and unwavering commitment to the betterment of society.

A Glimpse into Daily Life: Traditions and Customs of the Past

To truly understand the cultural heritage of the Republic of San Marino, one must delve into the customs and traditions that shaped the daily lives of its people in the past. Throughout history, the republic's inhabitants adhered to a rich tapestry of rituals and practices that defined their identity and celebrated their unique heritage.

In the medieval era, San Marino's daily life revolved around agriculture and craftsmanship. The rugged terrain of the Apennine Mountains presented both challenges and opportunities for its citizens. Agriculture played a vital role in sustaining the population, with farming practices adapting to the mountainous landscape.

Cultivating crops such as wheat, barley, and grapes, the people of San Marino relied on their agricultural prowess for sustenance and trade. Vineyards thrived on the sunlit slopes of Mount Titano, producing local wines that became prized commodities for trade and consumption.

The craftsmanship of San Marino's artisans was another cornerstone of daily life. From skilled blacksmiths to talented potters, artisans crafted essential tools, utensils, and ceramics that were integral to the daily routines of the people.

In addition to practical craftsmanship, the republic's artisans also excelled in producing religious artifacts and artistic works that adorned churches and palaces. San Marino's artistic legacy thrived, with local painters, sculptors, and musicians contributing to a vibrant cultural scene.

The religious calendar played a significant role in shaping daily life in San Marino. The republic's citizens were devoutly religious, and the church served as the center of communal life. Saints' feast days, religious processions, and ceremonies punctuated the year, bringing together the community in shared reverence and celebration.

Among the most significant religious celebrations was the Feast of Saint Marinus, the republic's patron saint. Held on September 3rd, this festival honored the founder of San Marino and featured processions, liturgical services, and communal feasts.

The traditional costume of San Marino was a prominent symbol of its cultural identity. In the past, both men and women donned distinctive attire that varied based on social status and occasion. The traditional dress showcased the republic's colorful heritage and regional diversity.

Hospitality was a cherished value in San Marino's daily life. Visitors were welcomed with open arms, and hosts took pride in offering generous hospitality to guests. Communal meals, marked by hearty dishes of regional cuisine, fostered a sense of camaraderie and warmth.

San Marino's cuisine is a delightful reflection of its past, blending flavors and influences from neighboring regions. Local dishes featured an array of ingredients, including fresh vegetables, meats, and cheeses. The republic's culinary heritage included specialties such as piadina, a flatbread filled with savory or sweet ingredients, and cacciatello, a traditional cheese.

Music and dance were essential elements of social life in San Marino. Festive gatherings and cultural events often featured traditional music and folk dances, providing moments of joy and entertainment for all generations.

Family values and close-knit communities played a crucial role in San Marino's daily life. Strong family ties and community bonds ensured mutual support and cooperation, especially in times of challenges and celebrations.

The republic's dedication to democracy and communal governance also left an indelible mark on daily life. The Grand and General Council, where every male citizen had a voice, shaped the republic's policies and decisions, fostering a sense of responsibility and civic engagement among its inhabitants.

As the years passed, and the world evolved, some of these traditions and customs gradually evolved as well. The advent of modern technology, advancements in communication, and changes in societal values contributed to a transformation in daily life in San Marino.

Yet, even in the face of change, the republic's commitment to preserving its cultural heritage remains strong. Traditional festivals, artistic expressions, and culinary delights continue to be cherished and celebrated, ensuring that the customs and traditions of the past continue to thrive in the present.

The Secret of Longevity: How San Marino Maintained its Independence

The Republic of San Marino's longevity as an independent nation is a fascinating tale of resilience, diplomacy, and strategic foresight. Nestled in the Apennine Mountains, this small landlocked state has managed to retain its sovereignty for over 1,700 years, making it one of the oldest continuously existing sovereign states in the world.

San Marino's secret to maintaining independence lies in a combination of unique factors and strategic decisions that have shaped its history. One of the key elements contributing to the republic's longevity is its geographic location. Situated atop the rugged peaks of Mount Titano, San Marino's mountainous terrain provided a natural advantage for defense. The rocky landscape made it challenging for invaders to conquer, and the steep slopes acted as a formidable deterrent to potential aggressors.

Moreover, the strategic location of San Marino, nestled in the heart of the Italian Peninsula, allowed it to navigate the complex geopolitical landscape of the region. Surrounded by larger and more powerful states, the republic chose a path of neutrality and diplomatic engagement, avoiding entanglements in the frequent feuds and conflicts that characterized medieval Italy.

San Marino's status as an independent republic can be traced back to its founding in AD 301 by Saint Marinus. Legend has it that Marinus, a Christian stonecutter fleeing persecution, sought refuge on Mount Titano and founded a small community based on principles of liberty and communal governance. The establishment of this small community laid the foundation for the independent republic that exists to this day.

Throughout its history, San Marino consistently maintained a policy of diplomatic neutrality. The republic's leaders recognized the importance of safeguarding its independence by avoiding alliances that could embroil it in external conflicts. This neutral stance earned San Marino the respect of neighboring states, allowing it to exist as a non-threatening entity in a volatile region.

The adoption of the Statuti, the republic's first written laws, played a crucial role in preserving its independence. The Statuti established a legal framework that promoted fairness, justice, and democratic governance, ensuring that power was vested in the hands of its citizens. This commitment to democratic principles contributed to the stability and continuity of the republic's governance.

San Marino's emphasis on a communal form of governance also fortified its independence. The republic's political system is characterized by a collective decision-making process, where all male citizens participate in the Grand and General Council. This inclusive approach ensured that the interests of the people were protected, fostering a sense of unity and shared responsibility for the preservation of independence.

Throughout its long history, San Marino faced external threats from various quarters, yet its defensive fortifications and strategic alliances allowed it to repel invasions and maintain its autonomy. The Three Towers of San Marino, perched on Mount Titano, served as symbols of the republic's determination to protect its sovereignty. These fortifications, enhanced by the natural barriers of the mountainous terrain, deterred potential invaders.

Additionally, San Marino skillfully navigated through the complexities of the Italian Renaissance and the Age of Enlightenment, embracing the intellectual and cultural innovations of the time while preserving its unique identity. The republic's commitment to the values of humanism and enlightenment fostered a spirit of progress while remaining grounded in its traditions.

During the tumultuous era of the Napoleonic Wars, San Marino's independence faced significant challenges. However, through shrewd diplomacy and strategic concessions, the republic managed to preserve its autonomy, even securing recognition from Napoleon Bonaparte himself, who spared San Marino from French annexation.

In the modern era, the republic's dedication to neutrality and diplomatic engagement continued to be vital for preserving independence. During World War II, San Marino maintained its neutral stance, avoiding direct involvement in the conflict despite the proximity of the frontlines. This approach protected the republic from the devastation faced by many European nations during the war.

As the world evolved, San Marino adapted its governance and embraced modernization while cherishing its historical heritage. The republic's commitment to democratic principles and human rights further solidified its position as an independent state respected by the international community.

The Grand Council: Aspects of Early Republican Government

The Grand Council stands as a cornerstone of the Republic of San Marino's early republican government. Established in the 13th century, this governing body played a vital role in shaping the republic's political landscape and reinforcing its commitment to democratic principles.

The roots of the Grand Council can be traced back to the medieval era when San Marino was emerging as a sovereign entity. As the population grew and the need for collective decision-making became evident, the council evolved into a formal institution representing the voice of the people.

The Grand Council was a legislative assembly composed of all male citizens of San Marino who were of age and in good standing. This inclusive structure set the republic apart from other contemporary forms of governance, where power often resided in the hands of a privileged elite.

The council met regularly to deliberate on important matters concerning the state. Its sessions were open to all citizens, promoting transparency and accountability in the decision-making process. Citizens could voice their opinions, contribute to debates, and vote on issues, ensuring that governance was rooted in the will of the people.

One of the primary functions of the Grand Council was the election of the Captains Regents. The Captains Regents served as the heads of state and the highest authorities in the republic. They held office for a six-month term and were elected from among the members of the council. This rotational leadership allowed for a balance of power and prevented the concentration of authority in any single individual or group.

In addition to electing the Captains Regents, the Grand Council was responsible for appointing other key officials, such as the councilors and judges. These appointments were made based on merit and experience, ensuring that qualified individuals held positions of responsibility in the government.

The council operated on a system of checks and balances, with various committees and magistrates overseeing different aspects of governance. This division of authority served as a safeguard against the abuse of power and encouraged collaboration among different branches of government.

The Grand Council's role extended beyond legislative matters. It was also responsible for foreign policy and diplomatic affairs. The republic's commitment to neutrality and peaceful coexistence with neighboring powers required careful diplomacy, and the council played a crucial role in forging alliances and securing treaties.

As a testament to its democratic values, the Grand Council actively sought to protect the rights and liberties of its citizens. The Statuti, the first written laws of San Marino dating back to the 16th century, enshrined fundamental rights such as freedom of speech, protection from arbitrary arrest, and the right to a fair trial.

The council's commitment to the principles of justice and fairness was also evident in its judicial functions. The councilors, who served as judges, dispensed justice based on the law and evidence presented in trials. Their impartiality and dedication to upholding the rule of law contributed to the republic's reputation for a just and equitable legal system.

The Grand Council's sessions were characterized by a vibrant exchange of ideas and opinions. Debates were passionate and sometimes contentious, reflecting the diverse perspectives and interests of the citizens. However, the council's commitment to consensus-building and the greater good of the republic prevailed, fostering a sense of unity and purpose among its members.

Despite the passage of time and the evolution of governance, the Grand Council remains a fundamental institution in the Republic of San Marino. Today, the council continues to play a crucial role in the republic's governance, although its composition and responsibilities have evolved to meet the demands of modern society.

As a symbol of democratic governance, the Grand Council stands as a testament to the enduring power of collective decision-making and citizen participation. Its legacy of transparency, inclusivity, and accountability continues to inspire governments worldwide in their pursuit of representative and responsible governance.

The Changing Tides: Adapting to the Modern World

The Republic of San Marino, with its rich history spanning over 1,700 years, has experienced a remarkable journey of adaptation and evolution in the face of the changing tides of the modern world. As the world advanced, San Marino, nestled in the heart of the Italian Peninsula, navigated the challenges and opportunities brought forth by the currents of progress, technology, and globalization.

The early 19th century witnessed significant changes in Europe, with the Napoleonic Wars and the rise of nation-states altering the geopolitical landscape. San Marino faced the threat of annexation by neighboring powers, but through diplomatic finesse and strategic concessions, it managed to preserve its independence. The Congress of Vienna in 1815 formally recognized San Marino as an independent and neutral state, securing its position on the world stage.

The Industrial Revolution, which swept across Europe during the 19th century, brought profound transformations to societies and economies. San Marino, known for its agrarian and artisanal traditions, was not immune to the impact of industrialization. The republic adapted to the changing economic landscape, embracing new technologies and methods to improve agricultural productivity and diversify its economic activities.

In the early 20th century, San Marino faced the challenges of World War I. Despite its commitment to neutrality, the republic faced economic hardships due to disruptions in trade and resources. However, San Marino's resilience and resourcefulness enabled it to weather the storm and emerge with its sovereignty intact.

The interwar period witnessed a period of cultural renaissance in San Marino. The republic's commitment to education and the arts continued to flourish, fostering a vibrant intellectual and artistic scene. San Marino became a haven for artists, writers, and scholars seeking inspiration in its historical and natural beauty.

During World War II, San Marino again faced the challenges of remaining neutral amid the turmoil of global conflict. The republic's strategic location placed it near the frontlines, but through cautious diplomacy and adherence to neutrality, it managed to preserve its independence and avoid direct involvement in the war.

Following World War II, San Marino embarked on a journey of reconstruction and modernization. The republic invested in infrastructure, healthcare, and education, laying the foundation for a prosperous and inclusive society.

In the latter half of the 20th century, San Marino embraced the opportunities presented by the digital revolution and the rise of globalization. The republic leveraged technology to enhance governance, education, and business operations. E-government initiatives improved administrative efficiency and transparency, making it easier for citizens to engage with the government.

In the 21st century, San Marino continues to adapt to the challenges and opportunities of the modern world. It remains committed to maintaining its cultural heritage and democratic values while embracing innovation and progress. The republic has become a hub for tourism, attracting visitors from around the world with its historical sites, natural beauty, and vibrant cultural scene.

As a member of various international organizations, including the United Nations and the Council of Europe, San Marino actively engages in global affairs. It seeks to contribute to international cooperation and promote peace and stability in the world.

San Marino's commitment to preserving its independence and sovereignty remains steadfast, as it navigates the complexities of the modern geopolitical landscape. The republic continues to forge strategic alliances and partnerships while safeguarding its cherished traditions and identity.

Literary Treasures: San Marino's Contributions to the Written Word

Beyond its storied history and political significance, the Republic of San Marino boasts a rich literary heritage that has left an indelible mark on the world of letters. Despite its small size, this mountainous enclave has produced a diverse array of literary treasures that span across various genres and periods.

San Marino's literary tradition can be traced back to its medieval origins when scribes and scholars recorded the republic's history and legal customs in manuscripts. These early literary works, written in Latin and vernacular languages, laid the foundation for the republic's cultural identity and intellectual pursuits.

In the 16th century, San Marino experienced a cultural renaissance that saw the flourishing of literature and the arts. Poets, playwrights, and scholars emerged, contributing to the republic's growing literary scene. The Palazzo Pubblico, with its grandeur and artistic ambiance, became a haven for intellectuals and creative minds.

One of San Marino's literary treasures from this period is the "Fioretto di San Marino," a poetic composition celebrating the republic's founding legend. Written in the Italian language, this work became an emblem of national pride and identity, reaffirming the republic's place in history and literature.

The 18th century witnessed the publication of "Istoria della republica di San Marino" ("History of the Republic of San

Marino") by historian Giovanni Francesco Borghesi. This comprehensive historical account chronicled the republic's past, providing valuable insights into its political, social, and cultural evolution.

San Marino's commitment to education and intellectual inquiry continued to thrive in the 19th century. The establishment of the University of San Marino in 1985 further bolstered the republic's intellectual landscape, attracting scholars and fostering research across various disciplines.

The 20th century marked a period of literary diversity in San Marino. Writers such as Marino Moretti and Guido Ceronetti rose to prominence, contributing to the republic's literary tapestry with their novels, poetry, and essays. Moretti's works delved into the complexities of human nature, while Ceronetti's thought-provoking prose explored philosophical and existential themes.

San Marino's literary scene also celebrated the power of storytelling. Folk tales, passed down through generations, enriched the cultural fabric of the republic. These oral traditions preserved the republic's history, legends, and values, making them accessible to people of all ages and backgrounds.

In the realm of poetry, San Marino produced notable voices that resonated far beyond its borders. The verses of Vittorio degli Albertini and Mariagrazia Contin made an impact on the Italian literary scene, while Mario Tommasini's poignant poetry captured the emotions of the human experience.

The republic's dedication to preserving and promoting its literary heritage is reflected in the presence of libraries and cultural institutions. The State Library of San Marino, established in 1600, houses a valuable collection of manuscripts, rare books, and literary works, providing a treasure trove for scholars and researchers.

San Marino's literary contributions extend beyond its borders, with its writers engaging in international collaborations and literary exchanges. The republic has participated in literary festivals, book fairs, and cultural events, fostering a spirit of dialogue and exchange with writers and readers worldwide.

In modern times, the digital era has opened new avenues for literary expression in San Marino. Writers and poets now share their works on digital platforms, reaching global audiences and bridging cultures through the written word.

Chasing Freedom: San Marino's Role in the Struggle for Liberation

Throughout its long and storied history, the Republic of San Marino has not only safeguarded its own independence but also played a notable role in supporting the pursuit of freedom and liberation in the wider world. As a beacon of democracy and human rights, San Marino has been a steadfast advocate for the principles of liberty, equality, and self-determination.

San Marino's commitment to freedom can be traced back to its founding in AD 301, a time when religious persecution was rampant in the Roman Empire. Saint Marinus, a Christian stonecutter, fled from his homeland to escape persecution and sought refuge on Mount Titano. There, he established a small community based on principles of freedom and liberty, setting the foundation for the independent republic that exists today.

Throughout the medieval era, San Marino's commitment to freedom was evident in its policy of providing sanctuary to those seeking refuge from political and religious persecution. The republic became a safe haven for individuals and groups fleeing conflicts and oppressive regimes. San Marino's stance on religious freedom set an example for other European states, where religious persecution was prevalent.

The republic's dedication to freedom was further reinforced by the establishment of its legal system, known as the Statuti, in the 16th century. These laws enshrined the principles of justice, equality, and the protection of individual rights. The Statuti provided a framework for a just and equitable society, ensuring that the rights and liberties of citizens were safeguarded.

As the Enlightenment swept across Europe in the 18th century, San Marino embraced the ideals of reason and human rights. The republic actively engaged with the intellectual and philosophical currents of the time, fostering a climate of intellectual inquiry and tolerance.

In the 19th century, San Marino's commitment to freedom found expression in its stance on neutrality and peaceful coexistence. The republic chose not to engage in aggressive wars or conflicts, instead pursuing a policy of diplomacy and non-intervention. This commitment to neutrality was driven by a desire to protect its own independence and to advocate for the principles of peace and freedom on the international stage.

During World War II, San Marino faced the challenges of maintaining its neutrality amidst the turmoil of global conflict. Despite its small size and vulnerable position near the frontlines, the republic managed to avoid direct involvement in the war. San Marino's stance on neutrality earned it the respect of the international community, and it was one of the few European states that emerged from the war with its sovereignty intact.

In the post-war era, San Marino continued to champion the cause of freedom and self-determination on the global stage. The republic actively engaged with international organizations, advocating for human rights, democracy, and peaceful resolution of conflicts. San Marino's commitment to promoting freedom and justice earned it a seat at the table of international diplomacy.

In more recent times, San Marino has been an advocate for global cooperation and the protection of human rights. The republic has participated in United Nations initiatives and has supported international efforts to address global challenges such as climate change, poverty, and humanitarian crises.

San Marino's role in the struggle for liberation extends beyond its diplomatic endeavors. The republic has been an advocate for the rights of refugees and displaced persons, offering assistance and support to those in need.

The republic's dedication to freedom is also reflected in its efforts to promote education and cultural exchange. San Marino's commitment to fostering intellectual growth and intercultural understanding has made it a destination for scholars, artists, and thinkers from around the world.

Rise of the Captains Regents: An Era of Dual Leadership

In the annals of San Marino's history, the rise of the Captains Regents marks a pivotal era of dual leadership that has endured for centuries. The Captains Regents are the highest authorities in the republic, serving as the heads of state and the embodiment of the principles of shared governance and political balance.

The origin of the Captains Regents can be traced back to the 13th century when the republic's political structure was evolving. The Grand Council, representing all male citizens, sought to ensure a fair and balanced distribution of power. To achieve this, the council devised a system of dual leadership, whereby two Captains Regents were elected to jointly hold the executive office for a six-month term.

The election of the Captains Regents follows a well-defined process. In the months leading up to the end of their term, the outgoing Captains Regents convene a General Assembly, inviting eligible citizens to propose candidates for the upcoming term. The candidates undergo a vetting process to ensure their eligibility and suitability for the position.

On the day of the election, the councilors, who are members of the Grand Council, gather to cast their votes for the new Captains Regents. To be elected, a candidate must secure a majority of votes. If no candidate receives a majority, a run-off election is held between the two candidates with the most votes.

The dual leadership of the Captains Regents is based on the principles of checks and balances. Each Captain Regent possesses equal powers, and no single individual can unilaterally make decisions. This arrangement fosters a spirit of cooperation and consensus-building in the highest echelons of governance.

During their term in office, the Captains Regents preside over the sessions of the Grand and General Council. They lead debates on legislative matters and executive decisions, ensuring that the interests of the citizens are heard and represented.

The Captains Regents also act as the symbolic heads of state, representing the republic in ceremonial functions and diplomatic engagements. They welcome foreign dignitaries and ambassadors, symbolizing San Marino's commitment to international relations and diplomacy.

Despite their limited six-month term, the Captains Regents wield considerable influence during their tenure. Their collective decision-making and leadership skills are instrumental in guiding the republic through periods of change and challenges.

The tradition of dual leadership has endured through the centuries, remaining a fundamental aspect of San Marino's political system. The continuity of this system is a testament to its effectiveness in ensuring stability, accountability, and the preservation of democratic values.

The Captains Regents have played a significant role in shaping the republic's history. Throughout the years, they have steered the republic through various historical events, including periods of conflict, political upheavals, and socio-economic changes.

San Marino's commitment to dual leadership has not gone unnoticed by the international community. The republic's system of governance has been hailed as a model of political stability and democratic representation.

In modern times, the role of the Captains Regents has expanded to encompass a more proactive engagement with global affairs. The republic actively participates in international organizations, advocating for human rights, peace, and justice.

The dual leadership of the Captains Regents continues to inspire scholars, political scientists, and policymakers worldwide. The system's ability to balance power and foster cooperative governance stands as an enduring example of effective leadership.

From Monarchy to Republic: The Transitional Phases

The transition from monarchy to republic in San Marino represents a fascinating chapter in the republic's history, marking a pivotal moment in its political evolution. While the exact details of this transformation are shrouded in the mists of time, historical records provide valuable insights into the various phases that led to the establishment of the world's oldest surviving republic.

The origins of San Marino's political structure can be traced back to the early 4th century when Saint Marinus, a Christian stonecutter, sought refuge on Mount Titano to escape religious persecution in the Roman Empire. There, he established a small community that would later evolve into the Republic of San Marino.

During its early years, San Marino was likely governed by a communal system, with local assemblies and councils making collective decisions. The notion of shared governance and democratic principles formed the basis of this incipient political structure.

In the centuries that followed, San Marino's governing institutions evolved, reflecting influences from neighboring regions and broader historical trends. While it is unclear if a formal monarchy existed, the republic's political system likely consisted of a group of prominent individuals who provided leadership and guidance.

The establishment of the Grand Council in the 13th century marked a significant milestone in the transition from a vague communal system to a more organized form of governance. The Grand Council, composed of male citizens, played a crucial role in shaping the republic's political landscape and setting the foundation for a democratic republic.

By the 15th century, San Marino had firmly established itself as an independent republic. The republic's unique political structure and commitment to self-governance drew admiration from neighboring states, leading to diplomatic recognition and support for its sovereignty.

The absence of a formal monarch in San Marino set it apart from the prevailing political systems of its time. Instead, the republic embraced a system of collective leadership, where power resided in the hands of the people through representative institutions like the Grand Council.

While the transition from monarchy to republic was a gradual process, San Marino's commitment to democratic principles and the absence of a centralized authority laid the groundwork for a republican form of government. The republic's political evolution was shaped by its desire for self-determination and the preservation of individual liberties.

San Marino's historical archives provide glimpses into the transformational phases that contributed to the republic's shift from a vague communal organization to a well-defined democratic system. These phases were marked by a continuous refinement of the republic's political institutions, culminating in the establishment of a stable and enduring republic.

The republic's status as a sovereign state with its own legal system and distinct identity was confirmed through diplomatic treaties and agreements with neighboring powers. The Congress of Vienna in 1815 formally recognized San Marino as an independent and neutral state, solidifying its place on the world stage.

The transition from monarchy to republic in San Marino represents a triumph of democratic ideals and collective decision-making. The establishment of the Grand Council and the absence of a monarch set a precedent for democratic governance that continues to endure to this day.

San Marino's Natural World: Wildlife and Ecology

Nestled within the Apennine Mountains, the Republic of San Marino boasts a diverse and captivating natural world that has been preserved through the ages. Despite its small size, this mountainous enclave is home to a rich array of wildlife and ecosystems, making it a haven for nature enthusiasts and conservationists alike.

San Marino's geography is characterized by rugged terrain, with its highest point being Mount Titano, standing at 739 meters (2,425 feet) above sea level. The republic's landscape comprises rolling hills, deep valleys, and dense woodlands, providing a variety of habitats for its unique wildlife.

In terms of flora, San Marino is adorned with diverse plant species, each contributing to the country's ecological richness. The lower regions are graced with Mediterranean vegetation, including olive groves, vineyards, and aromatic herbs like rosemary and thyme. As one ascends the mountain slopes, oak and beech forests dominate the landscape, offering a habitat for a myriad of wildlife.

San Marino's forests are not only vital for biodiversity but also serve as important carbon sinks, contributing to the fight against climate change. The republic places a strong emphasis on forest conservation and sustainable management practices to ensure the preservation of these invaluable ecosystems.

Among the fascinating wildlife that calls San Marino home, several notable species deserve mention. The Italian wolf (Canis lupus italicus) is one of the most iconic inhabitants of the country's woodlands. Though elusive and rarely seen, their presence is a testament to the health and preservation of the ecosystem. Similarly, the elusive European wildcat (Felis silvestris) and the agile red fox (Vulpes vulpes) thrive in the republic's natural habitats.

Birdwatchers will delight in spotting a diverse range of avian species that either reside or migrate through San Marino. These include birds of prey such as the majestic golden eagle (Aquila chrysaetos), the peregrine falcon (Falco peregrinus), and the common kestrel (Falco tinnunculus). Additionally, songbirds like the nightingale (Luscinia megarhynchos), the European robin (Erithacus rubecula), and the charming blackbird (Turdus merula) fill the air with their melodious calls.

The republic's water bodies also play host to various aquatic species, adding to the biodiversity of the region. Rivers and streams are home to species like the native Italian stream frog (Rana italica) and the agile European water shrew (Neomys fodiens). In the country's numerous ponds and small lakes, amphibians such as the common toad (Bufo bufo) and the green frog (Pelophylax lessonae) find sanctuary.

San Marino's commitment to conservation is evident through its protected areas and nature reserves. The state has designated specific zones, such as the Parco Naturale del Monte Titano (Nature Park of Mount Titano), to safeguard its unique natural heritage. These protected areas provide essential sanctuaries for wildlife and contribute to the maintenance of ecological balance.

Additionally, the republic engages in various environmental initiatives to mitigate human impact on the natural world. Sustainable practices in agriculture, waste management, and energy consumption are promoted to reduce the ecological footprint and ensure the long-term well-being of both nature and society.

San Marino's commitment to environmental stewardship extends beyond its borders through international cooperation. The republic actively participates in global efforts to combat climate change, conserve biodiversity, and promote sustainable development.

As the world grapples with environmental challenges, San Marino's dedication to preserving its natural world sets an inspiring example for other nations. The republic's harmonious coexistence with its wildlife and ecosystems stands as a testament to the importance of conservation and the shared responsibility of safeguarding the planet's natural heritage.

A Taste of San Marino: Exploring the Country's Unique Cuisine

San Marino's cuisine is a delightful fusion of flavors, influenced by its geographical location and historical connections to neighboring regions. The country's culinary heritage is a reflection of its rich history, with traditional dishes passed down through generations, preserving the essence of San Marino's cultural identity.

One of the hallmark features of San Marino's cuisine is its emphasis on using fresh and locally sourced ingredients. The fertile soils and Mediterranean climate provide an abundance of produce, including tomatoes, olives, peppers, and a variety of herbs. San Marino's commitment to sustainable agriculture and organic farming practices ensures that its traditional dishes are not only delicious but also healthy and environmentally conscious.

A staple in San Marino's gastronomy is the piada, a traditional flatbread made from simple ingredients like flour, water, olive oil, and a pinch of salt. Piada is a versatile dish, often served with cold cuts, cheese, or as an accompaniment to hearty stews and soups.

San Marino's cuisine also features an array of delectable pasta dishes. One such dish is the strozzapreti, a hand-rolled pasta shaped like twisted ropes, often served with a rich tomato-based sauce and grated cheese. The passatelli, a unique pasta made with breadcrumbs, Parmesan cheese, and eggs, simmered in a savory broth, is another beloved traditional dish that warms the soul, especially during the colder months.

As a landlocked country, San Marino has a strong tradition of preparing dishes with freshwater fish sourced from its numerous streams and ponds. Trout is a popular choice, often grilled or marinated in local herbs and olive oil, providing a delightful taste of the region's natural bounty.

San Marino's cuisine reflects the influence of neighboring Italy, particularly in its love for cheese. The republic produces an assortment of artisanal cheeses, including the famous pecorino cheese made from sheep's milk. The local cheeses often find their way into various dishes, from pasta sauces to cheese platters, celebrating the country's dairy heritage.

The country's culinary heritage is also intertwined with religious celebrations and festivals. During Christmas and Easter, traditional sweets like the nidi di rondine (swallow's nest) and torciglione, a sweet bread filled with walnuts and almonds, are lovingly prepared to mark these special occasions.

Another beloved treat in San Marino is the bustrengo, a delicious dessert made from leftover bread, apples, dried fruits, and a sprinkling of cinnamon. The result is a mouthwatering cake with a delightful blend of textures and flavors, celebrating the resourcefulness of San Marino's culinary traditions.

San Marino's passion for wine is evident in its vineyards that dot the landscape. The republic boasts a number of wineries producing both red and white wines, with the most common grape varieties being Sangiovese and Trebbiano. The local wines are often enjoyed with meals, complementing the flavors of the dishes and adding to the conviviality of the dining experience.

In recent years, San Marino has embraced a growing trend of farm-to-table dining and gastronomic tourism. The republic's commitment to sustainability and locally sourced produce has garnered attention from food enthusiasts seeking authentic and wholesome dining experiences. The country's culinary scene has also seen the rise of innovative chefs who infuse traditional dishes with modern twists, presenting a delightful fusion of old and new flavors.

Tourist Delights: Must-Visit Sights and Attractions

San Marino, with its picturesque landscapes, rich history, and charming architecture, offers a plethora of tourist delights that captivate visitors from around the world. As the world's oldest surviving republic, the country boasts a wealth of historical and cultural attractions, providing a captivating journey through time.

1. The Three Towers of San Marino: One of the most iconic symbols of the republic, the Three Towers - Guaita, Cesta, and Montale - stand proudly atop Mount Titano. Dating back to the 11th century, these medieval fortresses offer breathtaking panoramic views of the surrounding landscapes and serve as a reminder of the country's ancient past.
2. Piazza della Libertà: Situated in the heart of San Marino's capital, this charming square is a vibrant hub of activity. Surrounded by historic buildings and elegant cafes, the square is an ideal spot for soaking in the local atmosphere and enjoying a leisurely stroll.
3. Basilica di San Marino: The grandeur of the Basilica di San Marino, dedicated to the patron saint of the republic, Saint Marinus, is a sight to behold. Its impressive neoclassical facade and exquisite interior artworks make it a must-visit for those interested in religious history and architecture.
4. The Government Palace: Overlooking the Piazza della Libertà, the Government Palace houses the country's governmental offices. Visitors can witness the changing of the guard ceremony, which adds a touch of pomp and tradition to the experience.

5.The Museum of Emigration: This unique museum explores the history of San Marino's diaspora, highlighting the contributions of emigrants to various parts of the world. The museum provides valuable insights into the republic's global influence and its diaspora communities.

6.The State Museum: Housed in the historic Palazzo Pergami Belluzzi, the State Museum showcases an impressive collection of art, artifacts, and historical objects that span the centuries of San Marino's history.

7.The Public Palace: A prominent landmark in San Marino, the Public Palace is an architectural gem that features stunning frescoes and houses the Grand and General Council chambers. Guided tours offer visitors a glimpse into the country's political institutions and history.

8.Montegiardino: One of the republic's nine municipalities, Montegiardino is a charming village with narrow streets, ancient churches, and traditional stone houses. The village provides a serene escape from the bustling capital and an opportunity to experience rural life.

9.The Crossbow Corps Museum: The Crossbow Corps is a historical military organization that has played a significant role in the republic's defense. The museum offers a fascinating look at the Corps' weaponry, uniforms, and history.

10.The Wax Museum: A fun and interactive attraction, the Wax Museum features lifelike wax figures depicting historical figures, celebrities, and scenes from San Marino's past.

11.Borgo Maggiore: Another picturesque municipality, Borgo Maggiore offers a scenic setting with quaint alleys, historical buildings, and breathtaking views of the surrounding countryside.

12.The Liberty Square Statue: Located in the heart of San Marino's capital, the Liberty Square Statue is a bronze monument symbolizing freedom and independence. It serves as a gathering point and a backdrop for various events and celebrations.

13. The Grand Canyon Water Park: For those seeking leisure and recreation, the Grand Canyon Water Park offers a day of fun with its water slides, pools, and various aquatic attractions.

14. The International Museum of Curiosities: A quirky and entertaining museum, it houses a collection of oddities and curiosities from around the world, making it a unique and unforgettable experience.

15. The Borgo Maggiore Cable Car: For breathtaking views and a thrilling ride, the Borgo Maggiore Cable Car takes visitors up to the charming hilltop village, providing a memorable experience.

16. The Rock of St. Leo: A short hike from the capital, the Rock of St. Leo offers a tranquil spot to enjoy nature and admire the countryside.

17. Rimini Beach: Although not located within the borders of San Marino, Rimini Beach in nearby Italy is a popular destination for sun-seekers and offers a refreshing escape during hot summer months.

18. The Cava dei Balestrieri: Witness the ancient art of crossbow shooting at this historical archery range, where the Crossbow Corps demonstrates its skills during special events.

19. The Medieval Festivals: Throughout the year, San Marino hosts vibrant medieval festivals, allowing visitors to step back in time and experience the republic's historical traditions and customs.

20. The Rimini Miniature Park: A short drive from San Marino, this park features miniature replicas of famous Italian and European landmarks, making it a fun and educational outing for the whole family.

21. The San Marino Grand Prix: Car racing enthusiasts can attend the San Marino Grand Prix, which takes place on the

nearby Imola circuit, bringing excitement and adrenaline to the region.

22. The Christmas Markets: During the holiday season, San Marino's Christmas markets offer a festive ambiance with charming stalls selling crafts, decorations, and local delicacies.

23. The Tower of Montale Nature Reserve: Nature lovers can explore the Tower of Montale Nature Reserve, a protected area with walking trails and rich biodiversity.

24. The Sant'Agata Feltria Truffle Festival: For foodies, the nearby village of Sant'Agata Feltria hosts an annual truffle festival, celebrating the region's culinary treasures.

25. The Philatelic and Numismatic Office: Stamp and coin enthusiasts will enjoy visiting this unique office, which issues commemorative stamps and coins representing the republic's historical and cultural heritage.

In conclusion, San Marino's tourist delights offer a captivating blend of historical landmarks, natural beauty, and cultural experiences. From its medieval fortresses and picturesque villages to its vibrant festivals and stunning landscapes, the republic invites visitors to embark on a journey of discovery and appreciation for its rich history and unique charm. Whether exploring the ancient Three Towers or savoring the local cuisine, visitors to San Marino are bound to create cherished memories and gain a deeper understanding of this enchanting and culturally rich republic.

City of Liberty: Exploring San Marino City's Historic Significance

San Marino City, the capital of the Republic of San Marino, is a city steeped in history and significance. Perched atop Mount Titano, this ancient city holds the distinction of being the world's oldest surviving republic, a title that speaks to its enduring commitment to liberty and self-governance.

The foundation of San Marino City dates back to the early 4th century when Saint Marinus, a Christian stonecutter, sought refuge on Mount Titano to escape persecution by the Roman Empire. With a small group of followers, he established a community that would later evolve into the sovereign state of San Marino.

The city's strategic location atop a rugged mountain offered natural defenses, and this, combined with its early commitment to independence and liberty, set the stage for the formation of a unique political entity. San Marino City became a refuge for those seeking freedom from external control, attracting like-minded individuals who valued self-determination and autonomy.

In the centuries that followed, San Marino City's population grew, and the city expanded its influence beyond its fortified walls. The city's governance evolved from a communal system to a more organized form of government, characterized by a council known as the Grand Council, which was established in the 13th century. This council became the cornerstone of San Marino's political structure, representing the collective will of the people.

Throughout its history, San Marino City faced challenges and threats from various external powers, including neighboring states and invading forces. However, the city's commitment to freedom and resilience allowed it to withstand these challenges and maintain its independence.

San Marino City's historic significance extends beyond its political heritage. The city's architecture reflects its rich past, with medieval fortifications, ancient churches, and charming cobblestone streets that evoke a sense of timelessness. The Three Towers - Guaita, Cesta, and Montale - stand as symbols of the city's medieval fortifications, offering panoramic views and a connection to the past.

The Basilica di San Marino, dedicated to the republic's patron saint, Saint Marinus, is a cultural and spiritual treasure. Its neoclassical facade and exquisite interior artworks showcase the city's religious history and artistic heritage. The Public Palace, overlooking the Piazza della Libertà, serves as a testament to the city's democratic traditions. This historic building houses the chambers of the Grand and General Council, where decisions that shape the republic's future are made.

The Government Palace, located nearby, adds to the city's grandeur with its imposing architecture and serves as the official residence of the Captains Regents, the dual heads of state. Beyond its historical landmarks, San Marino City is a vibrant hub of culture and festivities. Throughout the year, the city hosts various events and festivals that celebrate the republic's heritage, including medieval reenactments, traditional processions, and colorful parades.

San Marino City's commitment to preserving its heritage and promoting cultural exchange is evident in its numerous museums. The State Museum, housed in the Palazzo Pergami Belluzzi, showcases a vast collection of art and artifacts that provide insights into the republic's history. The Museum of Emigration highlights the contributions of San Marino's diaspora communities, fostering a connection with the global Sanmarinese community.

Visiting San Marino City is like stepping into a living history book, where the past and present intertwine to create a captivating experience for travelers and history enthusiasts alike. The city's unique status as a sovereign state within the borders of Italy, combined with its enduring commitment to liberty and democracy, makes it a destination unlike any other in the world.

In recent times, San Marino City has embraced its role as a cultural and diplomatic hub, fostering relationships with other nations and participating in international forums. Its commitment to peace and diplomacy aligns with the city's historical role as a place of refuge and liberty.

Today, as visitors explore the cobbled streets of San Marino City, they can marvel at its ancient walls and immerse themselves in a rich tapestry of history, culture, and the enduring spirit of liberty that has defined this city for centuries. San Marino City's historic significance continues to inspire and captivate, making it a destination of choice for those seeking to connect with the past and be part of a living legacy of liberty and self-governance.

Montegiardino: Unraveling the Charms of the Oldest Municipality

Nestled amidst the picturesque landscape of the Republic of San Marino, Montegiardino holds the distinction of being the oldest municipality in this small but storied nation. As visitors venture into this charming village, they are greeted with a sense of tranquility and a timeless ambiance that harkens back to centuries past.

Montegiardino's history dates back to the early medieval period when the first settlements took root on the slopes of Mount Titano. The name "Montegiardino" translates to "Garden Mountain," a fitting title for a village embraced by nature's beauty and characterized by its lush surroundings.

As one of San Marino's nine municipalities, Montegiardino has played a pivotal role in the republic's history and cultural heritage. While the exact founding date remains obscured by the mists of time, it is widely accepted that the village's roots stretch back to the 10th century.

The allure of Montegiardino lies not only in its historical significance but also in its enchanting architecture and well-preserved traditions. Walking through its narrow streets, visitors are treated to a delightful array of traditional stone houses, adorned with flower-filled balconies and charming courtyards. These structures stand as testaments to the village's enduring commitment to preserving its cultural heritage.

One of the most prominent landmarks in Montegiardino is the Church of San Marino in Fiorentino. This ancient church, dating back to the 14th century, showcases an eclectic mix of architectural styles, including Romanesque and Gothic elements. Inside, visitors can marvel at its exquisite frescoes and sacred art, creating a serene atmosphere for contemplation and spiritual reflection.

For nature enthusiasts, Montegiardino offers a haven of scenic beauty. Surrounded by verdant hills and verdant valleys, the village is an ideal destination for those seeking a tranquil escape from the bustling city life. The pristine landscapes provide ample opportunities for leisurely hikes and leisurely picnics, allowing visitors to connect with nature's wonders.

One of the village's cultural highlights is the annual Chestnut Festival, celebrated every October. This festival is a beloved tradition that brings the community together to honor the harvest season and pay homage to the chestnut, a symbol of abundance and prosperity. During the festival, the streets come alive with music, dance, and various culinary delights featuring chestnuts as the star ingredient.

Beyond its natural beauty and cultural celebrations, Montegiardino's warm and welcoming community leaves a lasting impression on visitors. The village's small population fosters a close-knit and friendly atmosphere, where locals are eager to share stories of their heritage and way of life.

Montegiardino's commitment to preserving its cultural legacy extends to its culinary traditions. The village boasts a handful of charming eateries that serve authentic Sanmarinese dishes, prepared with locally sourced ingredients. From traditional pastas to savory stews, visitors can indulge in the flavors of the region while savoring the genuine hospitality of the village.

The village's historic significance and captivating charm have not gone unnoticed by travelers seeking a more intimate and off-the-beaten-path experience. Montegiardino has emerged as a hidden gem, inviting visitors to immerse themselves in its timeless allure and become part of its living history.

Preservation efforts in Montegiardino are taken seriously by both the local community and the government of San Marino. The village's historical buildings are carefully maintained, ensuring that their architectural heritage remains intact for generations to come.

Borgo Maggiore: Tracing the Growth of an Ancient Village

Nestled in the northeastern part of the Republic of San Marino, Borgo Maggiore is a captivating village that weaves together a tapestry of history, culture, and natural beauty. Its name, which translates to "Major Village," reflects its significance as one of the nine municipalities that constitute the republic.

The history of Borgo Maggiore dates back to ancient times, making it one of the oldest settlements in San Marino. While its exact founding date remains shrouded in the mists of time, archaeological evidence suggests that the village's origins can be traced back to the Roman era. Ancient artifacts and remains unearthed in the area offer glimpses into Borgo Maggiore's early life and its role as a trading post along the ancient Roman roadways.

Borgo Maggiore's strategic location on the eastern slopes of Mount Titano made it a crucial outpost for defending the republic's borders and safeguarding the capital city, San Marino. Its elevated position also provided a vantage point to monitor the surrounding territories, ensuring the security of the entire region.

As the republic of San Marino flourished and expanded over the centuries, Borgo Maggiore's significance grew in parallel. The village developed as a center of commerce and trade, serving as a hub for merchants and artisans who flocked to the region. Its bustling marketplaces and workshops became emblematic of its vibrant and enterprising spirit.

The architecture of Borgo Maggiore echoes its storied past. The village features a mix of medieval, Renaissance, and Baroque structures, each with its unique charm and historical significance. Quaint stone houses line the narrow streets, exuding an old-world charm that transports visitors to a bygone era.

One of the most remarkable landmarks in Borgo Maggiore is the Church of Saints Peter and Paul. This ancient church, dating back to the 14th century, showcases a captivating blend of architectural styles, including Romanesque and Gothic elements. Inside, visitors can marvel at its ornate altars, religious artworks, and sacred relics, providing a glimpse into the village's religious heritage.

Borgo Maggiore's strong sense of community and cultural identity is evident in its various festivals and traditions. Throughout the year, the village comes alive with vibrant celebrations that honor its history, faith, and customs. The Feast of Saint Barbara, the patron saint of the village, is a particularly significant event that brings together locals and visitors alike in a jubilant display of devotion and merriment.

Another cherished tradition in Borgo Maggiore is the Palio dei Balestrieri, a medieval crossbow competition that dates back to the 15th century. This annual event showcases the village's ancient crossbow heritage and the skill of its crossbowmen, adding a touch of pageantry and excitement to the village's cultural calendar.

Borgo Maggiore's commitment to preserving its heritage is exemplified by its museums and historical sites. The Museum of the Memory of the People is a unique cultural institution that presents the village's history through artifacts, documents, and multimedia displays. The museum offers visitors a comprehensive understanding of Borgo Maggiore's past and its contributions to the wider Sanmarinese society.

Beyond its historical and cultural treasures, Borgo Maggiore is surrounded by breathtaking natural landscapes. The village's position on the slopes of Mount Titano offers panoramic views of the rolling hills and verdant valleys that stretch out before it. These scenic vistas attract nature enthusiasts and hikers who seek to explore the beauty of San Marino's countryside.

In recent years, Borgo Maggiore has embraced its role as a destination for tourists seeking an authentic and immersive experience. The village's hospitality sector has grown to accommodate visitors, with charming guesthouses, boutique hotels, and traditional trattorias offering a taste of local hospitality.

Fiorentino: A Tapestry of Heritage and Legends

Nestled in the northeastern part of the Republic of San Marino, Fiorentino is a quaint village that weaves together a rich tapestry of heritage, legends, and natural beauty. As one of the nine municipalities that make up the republic, Fiorentino holds a unique place in the history and cultural fabric of San Marino.

Fiorentino's history stretches back to ancient times, and its name is believed to derive from the Latin word "Florentia," which means "flourishing" or "blooming." This name aptly captures the essence of the village, which has flourished over the centuries with a vibrant community and a strong sense of identity.

Archaeological discoveries in the area reveal evidence of human settlements dating back to the prehistoric era, attesting to Fiorentino's ancient origins. As the centuries passed, the village grew in significance, becoming a vital center for agriculture, trade, and craftsmanship.

The natural beauty of Fiorentino is one of its most alluring features. Surrounded by rolling hills, lush valleys, and olive groves, the village enjoys a serene setting that beckons travelers to immerse themselves in the splendor of San Marino's countryside. The pristine landscapes provide ample opportunities for outdoor activities such as hiking, cycling, and leisurely picnics, allowing visitors to connect with nature's wonders.

Fiorentino's architecture reflects its storied past, with a blend of medieval, Renaissance, and Baroque styles that grace the village's streets. Traditional stone houses with terracotta rooftops, charming courtyards, and flower-filled balconies create a picturesque scene that evokes a sense of timelessness.

One of the village's architectural gems is the Church of St. John the Baptist. This ancient church, dating back to the 14th century, stands as a symbol of Fiorentino's religious heritage. Its Romanesque facade and ornate interior hold captivating religious artworks, including altarpieces and frescoes, which provide insight into the village's spiritual life throughout the centuries.

Fiorentino's cultural identity is deeply rooted in its legends and folklore. The village is home to several fascinating tales that have been passed down through generations. One such legend revolves around a mythical creature known as the "Buso della Rana," a giant frog that is said to have lived in the nearby Fosso della Rocca stream. The legend of the Buso della Rana adds an air of enchantment and mystery to Fiorentino's already captivating atmosphere.

Throughout the year, Fiorentino comes alive with traditional festivals and celebrations that honor its history and customs. The Feast of St. Leo is a cherished event that pays homage to the patron saint of the village. During this festive occasion, locals and visitors gather to partake in processions, religious ceremonies, and lively festivities that foster a sense of community and camaraderie.

Fiorentino's commitment to preserving its heritage is evident in its museums and cultural initiatives. The Museum of the History of the Territory offers a comprehensive exploration of the village's past through archaeological finds, historical artifacts, and interactive exhibits. The museum provides an immersive experience that allows visitors to delve deeper into Fiorentino's ancient roots and cultural evolution.

The village's warm and welcoming community contributes to its unique charm. Locals take pride in sharing their heritage and traditions with visitors, creating a sense of hospitality that makes one feel at home in this small but endearing village.

Fiorentino's proximity to San Marino City, the capital of the republic, allows visitors to easily explore the wider region and immerse themselves in the charms of both urban and rural life.

Acquaviva: Preserving the Medieval Essence

Nestled in the picturesque countryside of the Republic of San Marino, Acquaviva is a charming village that exudes the essence of medieval heritage. As one of the nine municipalities in the republic, Acquaviva has stood the test of time, preserving its historical character and cultural identity.

Acquaviva's history can be traced back to ancient times, and its name, which translates to "living water," pays homage to the abundance of springs and water sources that have sustained the village throughout the centuries. The village's strategic location on the eastern side of Mount Titano provided natural defenses and allowed it to flourish as a center of agriculture and trade.

The architecture of Acquaviva is a captivating blend of medieval and Renaissance styles, with traditional stone houses and narrow cobblestone streets that wind their way through the village. As visitors stroll through Acquaviva, they are transported to a bygone era, where time seems to stand still, and the past comes alive in the enduring structures that grace the landscape.

One of the most prominent landmarks in Acquaviva is the Church of San Tomaso, which dates back to the 11th century. This ancient church stands as a testament to the village's religious heritage, with its Romanesque architecture and religious artworks that adorn its interior. The church serves as a spiritual center for the community, hosting religious ceremonies and events that connect the villagers to their faith and traditions.

Acquaviva's commitment to preserving its medieval essence extends beyond its architecture and landmarks. The village's cultural heritage is celebrated through various festivals and traditions that take place throughout the year. The Feast of Saint Thomas, held on December 21st, honors the patron saint of the village with processions, religious rituals, and communal gatherings that bring the community together in joyful celebration.

The village's strong sense of community is evident in its hospitality and warmth towards visitors. Acquaviva welcomes travelers with open arms, inviting them to immerse themselves in the tranquility of its surroundings and experience the authentic Sanmarinese way of life.

The natural beauty that envelops Acquaviva adds to its allure. Surrounded by verdant landscapes, the village enjoys breathtaking views of the rolling hills and valleys that stretch out before it. This idyllic setting provides a serene escape from the hustle and bustle of modern life, allowing visitors to unwind and connect with nature's wonders.

Acquaviva's proximity to San Marino City, the capital of the republic, makes it an accessible destination for travelers seeking a glimpse into the region's medieval past. Its location also allows visitors to explore the wider region and discover the unique charms of each municipality within the republic.

The village's commitment to preserving its cultural and historical heritage is evident in its initiatives to maintain and restore its architectural treasures. Preservation efforts are taken seriously by both the local community and the government of San Marino, ensuring that Acquaviva's medieval essence remains intact for future generations to appreciate.

In recent years, Acquaviva has embraced its role as a destination for cultural tourism, inviting travelers to step back in time and immerse themselves in its medieval ambiance. The village's hospitality sector has grown to accommodate visitors, with charming guesthouses and family-run establishments that offer a taste of traditional Sanmarinese hospitality.

Serravalle: Where Nature Meets History

Nestled in the northern part of the Republic of San Marino, Serravalle is a captivating village that seamlessly marries the beauty of nature with its rich historical heritage. As one of the nine municipalities in the republic, Serravalle is a destination that beckons travelers to explore its enchanting landscapes and delve into its storied past.

The name "Serravalle" translates to "valley closed off by hills," a fitting description for a village surrounded by rolling hills and valleys that create a natural sanctuary. Its strategic location on the banks of the San Marino River provided the village with fertile land for agriculture, making it a vital center for farming and trade in the region.

Serravalle's history can be traced back to ancient times, with evidence of human settlements dating back to the pre-Roman era. Over the centuries, the village evolved and grew, eventually becoming an integral part of the Republic of San Marino.

One of the most iconic landmarks in Serravalle is the Rocca dei Guaita, a medieval fortress perched on the peak of Mount Titano. The fortress, also known as the Guaita Tower, is the oldest of the three towers that overlook the capital city, San Marino. Its commanding presence and panoramic views of the surrounding landscape make it a symbol of strength and resilience.

The architectural charm of Serravalle is evident in its well-preserved buildings and quaint streets. The village's medieval character is reflected in traditional stone houses adorned with flower-filled balconies and charming courtyards. As visitors meander through Serravalle's cobbled streets, they are transported to a bygone era, where time seems to slow down, and the past mingles with the present.

Serravalle's rich cultural heritage is celebrated through various festivals and traditions that pay homage to the village's history and customs. The Feast of Saint Marinus, held on September 3rd, is a significant event that honors the founder of the republic. The festivities include religious processions, cultural events, and lively gatherings that showcase the community's strong sense of identity and unity.

The village's close connection with nature adds to its allure. Surrounded by verdant landscapes and fertile fields, Serravalle enjoys breathtaking views of the countryside and the nearby Adriatic Sea. Nature enthusiasts can indulge in leisurely walks, birdwatching, and exploring the region's diverse flora and fauna.

Serravalle's commitment to preserving its natural beauty is evident in its efforts to maintain green spaces and protect the environment. The village embraces sustainable practices, contributing to the region's status as one of the greenest areas in San Marino.

In addition to its natural splendor, Serravalle is a destination for travelers seeking an authentic experience in the heart of the republic. The village's hospitality sector has grown to accommodate visitors, with charming guesthouses, family-run trattorias, and local artisans offering a taste of traditional Sanmarinese hospitality and craftsmanship.

The village's proximity to San Marino City allows travelers to easily explore the wider region and immerse themselves in the cultural and historical treasures that await in each municipality within the republic.

Serravalle's dedication to preserving its heritage and fostering a sense of community contributes to its reputation as a welcoming destination. Locals take pride in sharing their traditions and way of life with visitors, inviting them to become a part of the village's timeless story.

Conclusion

As we reach the end of this journey through the history of San Marino, we find ourselves immersed in a tapestry of ancient beginnings, medieval expansion, and cultural crossroads that have shaped the unique nation we know today.

San Marino's origins are shrouded in mystery, but archaeological evidence points to prehistoric settlements that laid the foundation for the republic's enduring legacy. The story of Saint Marinus, the founder and patron saint, is intertwined with the nation's identity, symbolizing the courage and determination that have defined San Marino throughout its history.

The medieval era witnessed the republic's expansion and the development of its distinct political system. The Grand and General Council, a representative body of citizens, played a pivotal role in the governance of the republic, ensuring a voice for the people in shaping their destiny.

Fortifications and defense strategies were crucial in safeguarding San Marino's independence amidst regional conflicts. The iconic three towers, perched on Mount Titano, stand as enduring symbols of the republic's resilience and determination to protect its freedom.

Throughout the centuries, San Marino encountered various civilizations, absorbing cultural influences and contributing to the wider world through its written word, art, and architecture. Monasteries and their role in shaping the country, along with the impact of Renaissance achievements, added layers to the republic's identity as a hub of intellectual and artistic achievements.

San Marino's dedication to liberty and independence is a testament to its unique constitution, evolving over the centuries to maintain a balance between tradition and progress. From monarchy to republic, the transitional phases underscore the adaptability and unity that have sustained the nation through challenging times.

The preservation of San Marino's heritage and traditions is evident in the rich culinary delights that reflect the country's diverse cultural influences. From its wildlife and natural landscapes to the warmth of its people, San Marino offers visitors a glimpse into a world where nature meets history, creating an unforgettable experience.

In conclusion, the history of San Marino is a story of a small nation that defied the odds, embracing its roots while embracing change and progress. It is a tale of courage, unity, and resilience, with a heritage steeped in tradition and a vision firmly set on the future. As we bid farewell to this journey through the centuries, we are reminded of the enduring spirit of San Marino, a nation that continues to stand tall as a beacon of liberty and an inspiration to the world. Let its history serve as a reminder that from humble beginnings, great legacies can emerge, and the quest for freedom and independence can withstand the test of time.

Dear Reader,

If you enjoyed this journey and found the content engaging and enlightening, I kindly request you to share your thoughts and experiences by leaving a positive review. Your feedback is invaluable to me, and it will help others discover the captivating world of San Marino through the pages of this book.

Once again, thank you for your time and attention. I hope this book has left you with a sense of wonder and appreciation for the fascinating history of San Marino.